Women
on the R.U.N. for
JESUS

"For where two or three are gathered together in
My name, I am there in the midst of them."

(Matthew 18:20)

HELEN CUMMINGS-HENRY

WestBow
PRESS
A DIVISION OF THOMAS NELSON

Unless otherwise noted, All "Scripture taken from the New King James Version®.
Copyright © 1982 by Thomas Nelson, Inc. Used by permission. All rights reserved."

THE HOLY BIBLE, NEW INTERNATIONAL VERSION®, NIV® Copyright © 1973,
1978, 1984, 2011 by Biblica, Inc.® Used by permission. All rights reserved worldwide.

WestBow Press books may be ordered through booksellers or by contacting:

WestBow Press
A Division of Thomas Nelson
1663 Liberty Drive
Bloomington, IN 47403
www.westbowpress.com
1 (866) 928-1240

ISBN: 978-1-4908-1398-1 (sc)
ISBN: 978-1-4908-1399-8 (e)

Library of Congress Control Number: 2013919623

Print information available on the last page.

WestBow Press rev. date: 3/6/2015

CONTENTS

R(IGHTEOUS)

Ezekiel 18:5-9
But if a man is just And does what is lawful and right; If he has not eaten on the mountains, Nor lifted up his eyes to the idols of the house of Israel, Nor defiled his neighbor's wife, Nor approached a woman during her impurity; If he has not oppressed anyone, *But* has restored to the debtor his pledge; Has robbed no one by violence, *But* has given his bread to the hungry And covered the naked with clothing; If he has not exacted usury Nor taken any increase, *But* has withdrawn his hand from iniquity *And* executed true judgment between man and man; *If* he has walked in My statutes And kept My judgments faithfully— He *is* just; He shall surely live!" Says the Lord GOD.

Jeremiah 17:8
For he shall be like a tree planted by the waters, Which spreads out its roots by the river, And will not fear when heat comes; But its leaf will be green, And will not be anxious in the year of drought, Nor will cease from yielding fruit.

Revelation 1:6
and has made us kings and priests to His God and Father, to Him *be* glory and dominion forever and ever. Amen.

1 John 3:6
Whoever abides in Him does not sin. Whoever sins has neither seen Him nor known Him.

Meditate on the Bible Verses on Righteous Living.
Apply (1) one of the Bible Verses to your life.
Paraphrase a verse that applies to you and discuss your thoughts.

U(PLIFTING)

Hebrews 13:5
Let your conduct *be* without covetousness; *be* content with such things as you have. For He Himself has said, "I will never leave you nor forsake you."

John 3:16
For God so loved the world that He gave His only begotten Son, that whoever believes in Him should not perish but have everlasting life.

1 Thessalonians 2:13
For this reason we also thank God without ceasing, because when you received the word of God which you heard from us, you welcomed *it* not *as* the word of men, but as it is in truth, the word of God, which also effectively works in you who believe.

Matthew 6:33
But seek first the kingdom of God and His righteousness, and all these things shall be added to you.

Meditate on the Bible Verses on Uplifting.

Apply (1) one of the Bible Verses to your life.

Paraphrase a verse that applies to you and discuss your thoughts.

N(OURISHING)

John 14:6
Jesus said to him, "I am the way, the truth, and the life. No one comes to the Father except through Me."

Psalm 23:1-6
The LORD *is* my shepherd; I shall not want. He makes me to lie down in green pastures; He leads me beside the still waters. He restores my soul; He leads me in the paths of righteousness For His name's sake.

Yea, though I walk through the valley of the shadow of death, I will fear no evil; For You *are* with me; Your rod and Your staff, they comfort me.

You prepare a table before me in the presence of my enemies; You anoint my head with oil; My cup runs over. Surely goodness and mercy shall follow me All the days of my life; And I will dwell in the house of the LORD Forever.

2 Corinthians 9:6-8
But thus I say: He who sows sparingly will also reap sparingly, and he who sows bountifully will also reap bountifully. So let each one must give as he purposes in his heart, not grudgingly or of necessity for God loves a cheerful giver. And God is able to make all grace abound toward you, that you having all sufficiency in all things, may have an abundance for every good work.

Meditate on the Bible Verses on Nourishing
Apply (1) one of the Bible Verses to your life.
Paraphrase a verse that applies to you and discuss your thoughts.

ACKNOWLEDGEMENTS

First, I thank my Lord and Savior, Jesus Christ for giving me another chance to continue writing and giving me the wisdom and knowledge to do so. I thank Him for letting me be a part of what is His will for my life.

I thank my mother, Beryl for talking to me about Jesus and having Christ in her life.

I thank my husband Arthur who is the editor of the book. I thank him for his encouragement and support.

I thank my children, Miguel and Edward for being there for me and encouraging me to continue to write.

I thank all of the Women on the R.U.N. for Jesus, past, present and future for their participation in the meetings, to God be the glory.

Lastly, I want to thank you who are reading this book, I don't know what you have been through, are going through but I pray that your life is being changed by divine appointment. Accept Christ as your Personal Lord and Savior and begin to build a relationship with Him.

Grace and Peace,

Helen - Your Sister in Christ

FOREWORD

From the Pen of – Tarrent-Arthur Henry

My spiritual daughters, you are about to embark on a spiritual journey that is about to change your life.

God has given Sister Helen an assignment, a mandate to be your Spiritual Trainer. You are about to be transformed daily by the renewing of your mind. God's Gym is no ordinary gym. So get ready daughters of the King to be strengthened spiritually through Christ. Whether you are the seed by the wayside, (Non-Believer), the seed in stony places, (Follower) or the seed sown amongst thorns, (Back-Slider);

Prepare yourself to be seed sown into good ground. See yourself as a branch attached to the Vine (Jesus) bearing much fruit. Are you ready to take that journey? This book was written from God's hand to Helen's heart with the blessed hope to minister to you; spirit, soul and body, to unite women of different ethnic backgrounds and bridge the gap between the believer and the non-believer to break down denominational walls, to open the doors of communication through divine fellowship and to provide the tools necessary for you to become the woman that God has called you to be.

As Pastor and Shepherd of this group, my prayer is that God will use my wife and your sister Helen as a tool to shape and mold you into a vessel fit for the Master's use. Please pray this prayer with me:

Lord Jesus, I Believe That You Are God. I Believe That You Went To The Cross To Die For Me. I Believe That You Rose From The Dead. Lord Jesus, I Am A Sinner And I Want To Repent Of My Sin. I Am Inviting You To Come Inside And Live In And Through Me. Right Now Jesus, Take Full Control Of My Life, Starting Today. In Your Precious Name I Pray, Amen and Amen. If you prayed that prayer for the first time, Welcome to the Family of God and to those who have prayed it before, you are about to be empowered to be strong in the Lord. A Woman on the **R**(ighteous) **U**(plifting) **N**(ourishing) for Jesus!

INTRODUCTION

When a baby is born, the baby starts to cry. The baby crawls and as the legs get strong and the baby is more confident, he/she starts to take first steps, which is walking. After the toddler gets more balance, the child starts to run.

Our relationship with God begins in a similar fashion. We are born, we cry, we crawl, we stand and as our Faith gets strong, we become more confident. We start to walk. My encounter with God happened like this:

I was raised by a strict father so I had to abide by the rules which weren't easy sometimes. However, I had to adjust. I was very quiet at times but there were times when anger would get the best of me, especially if someone spoke to me harshly. I was not allowed to do things like the average teenage boy or girl today; such as partying, dating, staying out late with friends, you name it. After the death of my earthly father, I began to develop worldly habits and fleshly ways. Not only did I do things my way, I paid the consequences for it. Then my girlfriend told me I had a Heavenly Father and I became a Christian Believer.

My struggles with everyday life led me to want to know Him. I got saved, water baptized and joined a local Church. However, I was not understanding the Bible. I would read it and read it, but still could not understand the text. I was a Christian believer but I was not strong in my walk with God. Over time, I began to understand and become hungry for Jesus. I took some classes and learned that Jesus is not a

Religion but a Relationship. Through those classes and my marriage to my husband Arthur, I have learned how to make the Word of God my Food for each day. Now I am a Woman on the R.U.N. for Jesus.

In February 2012, God birthed in my spirit, **"Women on the R.U.N. for Jesus"**. Immediately, I stepped out in faith and obeyed God. On March 3, 2012, **"Women on the R.U.N. for Jesus"** was born. Women on the R.U.N. (Righteous-Uplifting-Nourishing) began when I told my husband, God spoke to me, to call a few women who are hungry for Jesus and have them come to our home and have a Bible study. I then said to my husband, Arthur, what if no-one is interested. My husband then said to me, "well we both will sit and have the Bible study." (*For where two or three are gathered together in My name, I am there in the midst of them."*) Matthew 18:20.

We started with two women being hungry for Jesus and to God be the Glory, Women on the R.U.N. for Jesus is growing with more women being hungry for J E S U S. Thanks be to God.

Please pray along with me:

Heavenly Father, I thank you. I thank you for giving me the wisdom to reach out to the world. Lord, I give you the praise. I give you the glory. I give you the honor. I worship you O Lord, for you are Sovereign in my life. You are Alpha and Omega. Lord, I thank you for directing my steps and having mercy on me because I know that I am not perfect. I need you Father, in my life each and every day. I know there is always something in me that you are working on and I surrender all to you. I acknowledge Father, that I am not always pleasing to you, but because you are Wonderful, because you are Merciful, I know that your love is everlasting. I thank you Father for purifying my mind and using me in whatever way that is pleasing to you and forgive me Father for anything that is not pleasing to you. Lord, I thank you for allowing me to renew my mind each and every day so that I can hear more from you. I pray this prayer, in Jesus name. Amen.

CHAPTER 1

(Unsaved) - Women on the R.U.N. for JESUS

Let's begin our lesson by opening our Bible to the Book Of *John* and <u>read</u> *Chapter 4 verses 1-42.*

St. John 4:1-42 will be the foundation that <u>Women on the R.U.N. for Jesus is</u> built on.

"In early New Testament times women gathered at the well, drawing water and talking to one another about their lives and probably helping to advise each other about the problems or dilemmas in their lives. But one woman went to the well when she knew the others would not be there because of her shameful lifestyle that was unacceptable.

She waited until much later and went thinking she would avoid a confrontation with those who she knew would avoid her and look on her with disdain. But along came Jesus who knew when she would be there and brought along understanding, compassion, and love. He left out condemnation and judgment and instead brought God's Riches At Christ's Expense.

It was this encounter that changed her life and her lifestyle."

The purpose and the vision of Women on the R.U.N. for Jesus:

- *To minister to the total woman (spirit, soul and body).*
- *To gather women from different ethnic backgrounds and Christian denominations.*
- *To open the doors of communication through fellowship.*
- *To provide the tools necessary to become the Women that God has called us to be.*

Why are so many people still Unsaved?

Second Corinthians 4:4 tells us it is because "the god of this world [the devil] hath blinded the minds of them which believe not, lest the light of the glorious gospel of Christ, who is the image of God, should shine unto them."

Once you realize it's the devil (not your loved one) who's the real problem, your first prayer step becomes clear. You must get the devil out of your loved one's way. As Jesus said, "How can one enter into a strong man's house, and spoil his goods, except he first bind the strong man?" (Matthew 12:29). You can't! So bind him.

Now, you may not be able to cast that devil entirely out of the situation, because your loved one may invite him back in faster than you can cast him out. But you *can* bind that spirit and keep it bound. It may keep you busy for a while, but you can do it.

Verbal (say out loud) Confession of Faith in God's help to save loved one:

> God is not willing that this person (name the person) perish, but that he or she comes to repentance – 2 Peter 3:9.

> It is God's will that he or she (name the person) be saved and comes to a knowledge of truth – 1 Timothy 2:4.

> This is the confidence that I have in Him, that if I ask anything according to His will, He hears me. And I know that if He hears me, whatever I ask, I know that I have the petitions that I have asked of Him. I ask for him or her (name the person) to be saved, to come to repentance, and to come to a knowledge of the truth that can set him or her free – 1 John 5:14, 15.

> If it is a relative: I believe that I and all of my household will be saved – Acts 16:31.

> I realize that I am not in a battle with flesh and blood, but I am contending against demonic powers, wicked spirits in the heavenly sphere, who are trying to influence and control the person I am praying for – Ephesians 6:12. Jesus said in Luke 10:19, "I give you authority and power over all the power of the enemy "and so nothing shall in any way harm me.

Whatever I bind on earth is bound in the heavenly realm, and whatever I loose on earth is loosed in the heavenly realm – Matthew 18:18.

Binding prayer (2 Corinthians 4:3,4):

Say, "Right now I bind the god of this world (Satan) who has blinded their eyes to the truth of the gospel, and I loose the light of the gospel to shine on them and open their eyes. You spirit operating in the life of my loved one, blinding __(name the person)___ to the gospel to keep __(name the person)_____ out of the kingdom of God, I bind you now. I belong to the Lord Jesus Christ. I carry His authority and righteousness and in His Name, I command you to desist in your maneuvers. I spoil your house according to the Word of God and I enter into it to deliver my loved one from your hands."

I pray that the eyes of their understanding would be opened to know the hope of their calling – Ephesians 1:18.

> Lord, open their eyes to know You; open their understanding that they can understand the scriptures – Luke 24:31, 45.

> I pray for laborers to be sent into their path from the Lord of the harvest – Matthew 9:37, 38.

> I believe that I receive the answers to these scriptural prayers – Mark 11:24.

> Lord, You watch over Your Word to perform it – Jeremiah 1:12.

> Thank You that Your Word does not return to You void, but it accomplishes what You intend for it to do – Isaiah 55:11.

Meditate:
Matthew 18:18-20

Pray:
I am inviting all "Women on the R.U.N. for Jesus" to spend a minimum of one (1) hour daily in prayer.

Read:
Matthew 18 for discussion.

CHAPTER 2

Grace, Faith and Patience

Let's begin our lesson by opening our Bible to the Book Of *John* and <u>read</u> *Chapter 4 verses 1-42.*

St. John 4:1-42 will be the foundation that <u>Women on the R.U.N. for Jesus</u> is built on.

Pam and Dan

When I met Pam and her husband Dan, I really admired them. They were the ideal couple. They had it all. When I said, had it all, they lived in a large five bedroom home in the Westchester Area of upstate New York. They frequently travelled to many countries, enjoying the different sites and living life like it's golden.

One day I sat down with Pam and while conversing with her. I asked her, "Girl, would you like to get to know Jesus"? She looked at me and said, "I go to Church sometimes." "I believe in God." Then I said, "But are you a Christian, sis?" "Would you like to have a personal relationship with Jesus?" She said, "I am so busy, girl." "I pray and I know God answers my prayers." "I travel and I work hard, I know God is with me." "I am a hard working woman and my husband is a hard working man, we give money to the church and God is blessing us."

You see, sometimes we get caught up in the material stuff in the world and do not care to know Jesus. Jesus is the one providing for us. Jesus is the one that gave His life so that you might live. Jesus is the one that took off His royal crown and exchanged it for a crown of thorns. Why can't we spend more time with Jesus? Why isn't Jesus paramount in our life?

Pam and her husband Dan were so involved in enjoying the fancy living. The lavish lifestyle but not spending time to know Jesus and having a relationship with Him. One afternoon, Pam called me and told me that Dan had lost his high paying job as a Manager for the company he worked for twenty years. She said to me, "What are we going to do?" "My income will not be able to take care of this house." "We are tied up in credit card debt." "We have a mortgage to pay." "What are we going to do, sis?"

I said to her, "Material stuff will pass away but God's Word is everlasting." She started to cry, "Lord, I am so sorry for not spending time with you and getting to know your Word." "Have mercy on me Father." "I got caught up in enjoying the things of this world." "Help me Father, I want to have a closer walk with you." "I want to have a relationship with you, Jesus." "Please, help us Lord."

Pam and Dan started going back to a neighborhood Church and accepted Jesus Christ as Lord and Savior. They served in Church and spent quality time in the Word. After spending more time in the Word and getting to know God and not relying on their own understanding, the house, the job and the material stuff that they had gotten caught up in was restored.

God blessed Dan with a job that was able to help pay off the mortgage and debt that was owed. They sold their house and bought a smaller house and are enjoying and spending more time in serving God.

The Bible says: "Therefore I say to you, do not worry about your life, what you will eat or what you will drink, nor about your body, what you will put on. Is not life more than food and the body more than clothing?" (Matthew 6:25).

We sometimes worry about things of the world. We put our focus on what is going to happen tomorrow when we should be focusing on God, our source. He is the one who provides for us and will continue to do so. He will never leave us nor forsake us.

When we come to know Jesus, we must be able to focus on Him more than the materialistic stuff of this world. Spending time with Jesus and getting to know Him as your Personal Savior and having a relationship with Him is so important. You can call on Him anytime. He will be there. Having Faith and believing that He is able to do anything but fail.

Are you serving God with your whole spirit, soul and body?

How do I do that you might ask?

You have to change your thoughts, decisions and actions to agree with His.
You must conform to God's will and not the ways of this world.
You must put yourself into obedience to every Word and every Command of God.

God's Word comes in (2) two ways . . . .

(1) By His Written Word and (2) By the Holy Spirit speaking to our spirit.

THE HOLY SPIRIT WILL NEVER LEAD YOU CONTRARY TO THE WORD OF GOD

I challenge you to say and make this simple declaration:

Holy Spirit teach me how to follow you. Take control of every area of my life Holy Spirit and reveal the will of God for my life, step by step.

I give you my personal guarantee that if you give Him every ounce of your attention.

If you give Him your total obedience.

God will - Introduce your husband to you.
God will - Open your barren womb.
God will - Restore and strengthen your marriage.
God will - Break the chains of physical, mental and emotional abuse.
God will - Grant you favor in the job market.
God will - Restore your family.
God will - Interpret your dreams.
God will - Joel 2:25-26.

Whatever it is . . . . Believe God by Grace-Faith and Patience.

We have absolutely no excuse not to face each and every situation with CONFIDENCE.

Meditate:
Matthew 18:18-20

Pray:
I am inviting all "Women on the R.U.N. for Jesus" to spend a minimum of one (1) hour daily in prayer.

Read: Romans Chapter 10 for discussion.

CHAPTER 3

The Well Of Jacob

Let's begin our lesson by opening our Bible to the Book Of *John* and <u>read</u> *Chapter 4 verses 1-42*.

St. John 4:1-42 will be the foundation that <u>Women on the R.U.N. for Jesus</u> is built on.

Go with me to the Book of John 4:1-6: *Jesus knew the Pharisees had heard that He was baptizing and making more disciples than John (though Jesus himself didn't baptize them—His disciples did). So he left Judea and returned to Galilee.*

He had to go through Samaria on the way. Eventually he came to the Samaritan village of Sychar, near the field that Jacob gave to his son Joseph. ***Jacob's well*** *was there; and Jesus, tired from the long walk, sat wearily beside the well about noontime.* Jesus stopped and sat by the **Well of Jacob *(the Supplanter)*.** *Supplanter is one who takes the place or moves* *into the position of another. Jacob was known as the supplanter for what he perpetrated on Esau. (See Genesis 25:29-33).* Now let's continue from verse 7: *Soon a Samaritan woman came to draw water, and Jesus said to her, "Please give me a drink." He was alone at the time because his disciples had gone into the village to buy some food. The woman was surprised, for Jews refuse to have anything to do with Samaritans. She said to Jesus, "You are a Jew, and I am a Samaritan woman. Why are you asking me for a drink?" Verse 10:* Jesus replied, *"If you only knew the gift God has for you and who you are speaking to, you would ask me, and I would give you living water."* **God has a gift for you . . . . . God has a gift for you . . . .** Verse 11: *"But sir, you don't have a rope or a bucket,"* she said, *"and this well is very deep. Where would you get this living water? And besides, do you think you're greater than our ancestor Jacob, who gave us this well? How can you offer better water than he and his sons and his animals enjoyed?"*

We must learn to get out big buts out of the way and learn not to place a question mark where God has placed a period. Verse 13: *Jesus replied, "Anyone who drinks this water will soon become thirsty again. But those who drink the water I give will never be thirsty again. It becomes a fresh, bubbling spring within them, giving them eternal life."* Does anybody reading this want **Eternal Life?** Verse 15: *"Please, sir," the woman said, "give me this water! Then I'll never be thirsty again, and I won't have to come here to get water." Verse 16: "Go and get your husband," Jesus told her. "I don't have a husband," the woman replied. Jesus said, "You're right! You don't have a husband—for you have had five husbands, and you aren't even married to the man you're living with now. You certainly spoke the truth!"* Are you in an adulterous relationship? Are you searching for a husband instead of looking to Jesus? Are you harboring unforgiveness in your heart? Are you where God wants you to be?

Meditate:
Matthew 18:18-20

Pray:
I am inviting all "Women on the R.U.N. for Jesus" to spend a minimum of one (1) hour daily in prayer.

Read: 1 Corinthians Chapter 12

CHAPTER 4

Focusing On God

Let's begin our lesson by opening our Bible to the Book Of *John* and <u>read</u> *Chapter 4 verses 1-42.*

St. John 4:1-42 will be the foundation that <u>Women on the R.U.N. for Jesus </u>is built on.

God does not want you to focus on what is going on in your life. He wants you to prosper and be in health even as your soul prospers. God has a wonderful plan for your life.

I like to take this opportunity to thank my husband . . . . You see the devil tried to attack me one afternoon . . . . . . Let me explain . . . . I was preparing my Sunday dinner and some hot oil flew in my eye and I had been unable to see clearly . . . . but devil . . . . . I'm putting you on notice . . . . I bind you from this classroom and I loose my healing (by His stripes) . . . .

. . . . . Hallelujah . . . And devil I give you a black eye. We (my husband and I) took authority over the enemy and told him where to go . . . Hallelujah . . . . Ha, Ha, Ha, devil, you got to flee right now in the Name of Jesus because I am covered by the blood of the Lamb and my testimony. Do I have a witness in the house . . . . . that know . . . that they know . . . that they know? The devil is a liar! He tried very hard to keep this message from getting out . . . . . . but glory to God . . . . . It is done! My eyes are healed and I am delivered . . . . The devil tried to take my joy. Ha, Ha, but he failed again. You see, my sisters, please, do not let <u>anyone</u>, I said <u>anyone</u> take your joy from you, because the joy of the Lord is your strength.

First to begin with, I always start out by putting God first in everything I do and I will like to take this moment just to thank Him and call His name. Please pray along with me:

Heavenly Father, I thank you. I thank you for giving me the wisdom to reach out to the world. Lord, I give you the praise. I give you the glory. I give you the honor. I worship you O Lord, for you are Sovereign in my life. You are Alpha and Omega. Lord, I thank you for directing my steps and having mercy on me because I know that I am not perfect. I need you Father, in my life each and every day. I know there is always something in me that you are working on and I surrender all to you. I acknowledge Father, that I am not always pleasing to you, but because you are Wonderful, because you are Merciful, I know that your love is everlasting. I thank you Father for purifying my mind and using me in whatever way that is pleasing to you and forgive me Father for anything that is not pleasing to you. Lord, I thank you for allowing me to renew my mind each and everyday so that I can hear more from you. I pray this prayer, in Jesus name. Amen.

When God speaks to you about something that you should do, you should not ask another person. God already spoke to you. You should do what He says. We sometimes call up others and speak to them about what they think. If God assigns you to do something. Do it. You do not have to get another's approval. There are many times in my life where I ask another's opinion in what God has already spoken to me about. You see, when we come to understand clearly that God is a jealous God and that He comes first, we will not want to hear another's opinion. Having that intimate relationship with Jesus is all that matters. When we get into His presence and His Word, He will show us what we need to know. There were times, I was so sick and tired of asking this one and that one about something God had already spoken to me about. **In James 1:19,** *so then my beloved brethren, let every man be swift to hear, slow to speak, slow to wrath.* Being quick to listen and slow to speak is what God requires of us. We need to just listen to that still small voice and speak what is pleasing to God. I remember many times when, oops, I was quick to speak and it was not a good feeling to know that some of my words did not edify God. My spirit was not feeling right. I realize the tongue can be quick to speak. I acknowledged that I was wrong, repented to God and asked His mercy. When we acknowledge and know that we are totally wrong we must go directly and speak to God and let Him know we messed up. He will forgive you.

Lord, I lift up every woman and their families in this class that I am about to teach in the Name of Jesus. Lord, I ask that they come to you with a clean heart, a loving heart, a forgiving heart. Lord, help them to keep the Focus on you Father. Touch their hearts Father. Lord you know each and everyone's needs. Healing for pain in the knee. Healing for foot ache. Healing for headache. Healing for their children, loved ones. Whatever the need is, Father. I come to you in agreement with each of these women today that all their needs will be met, in the Name of Jesus. Amen.

When we spend time with God and not worry about the everyday tasks in our life, God will begin to speak through His Word of what is His Will for our life. God's Word is His will." *'For I know the plans I have for you,' declared the Lord, 'plans to prosper you and not to harm you, plans to give you hope and a future'"* (Jeremiah 29:11).

God is love, so his plan for you is always good. He will never leave you nor forsake you. He is always on time. You must be patient. Do not worry about tomorrow, let tomorrow take care of itself. Sometimes, we get ahead of God because we want things to happen right away. Do I have a witness in the house that sometimes you are tired of waiting for what you ask for from God? You expect things to happen in your time and when it does not happen you get upset, confused and emotional. But God works everything out for our good. It will not happen in your time, but God's time is always the best time. God's will is always pleasing, good and perfect. We must trust in His Word. His Word also says: *Trust in the Lord with all your heart and lean not on your own understanding; in all ways acknowledge Him, and He will make your paths straight"* (Proverbs 3:5-6).

To discern God's Will for our lives, we must ask God to give us wisdom. He will give it to us. His Word says: *"If any of you lacks wisdom, let him ask God, who gives to all liberally and without reproach, and it will be given to him"* (James 1:5).

My sisters in Christ, I don't know where God is going to take us, but I am obedient to the Lord and allowing Him to move in each and every one of our lives as we journey forth together to Praise Him and do what is pleasing to Him.

I want to start out by asking each and every one of you to examine yourself and see where you are in Christ. Are you focusing on your problem? Are you focusing on the material things of the world? Are you focusing on getting married? Are you focusing on having a better job? Are you focusing on having a house? Are you focusing on a financial blessing? Whatever, the focus, I ask you to begin focusing now on **Jesus.** Forget about all your needs right now and put your **Focus on Jesus**. When you begin to obey the Word. When you begin to speak to **Jesus.** When you begin to renew your mind each and every day by taking in new information from the Word. When you choose to be obedient and focus more on Him above anything in your life right now . . . . You will always have the assurance that **Jesus** will never leave you nor forsake you in any issue or problem that is going on in your life right now or in the future. Jesus Christ, the same today, yesterday and forever.

You see, my Christian sisters, Jesus is the Lover of My Soul. Though our world may fail at times, we should never let Him go, He is our Savior, He is our Friend, and we should be worshiping Him until the very end.

Meditate:
Matthew 18:18-20

Pray:
I am inviting all "Women on the R.U.N. for Jesus" to spend a minimum of one (1) hour daily in prayer.

Read: Luke 8:43-48

See yourself in this passage of scripture?
What lesson(s) has the Holy Spirit taught you?
I would love to hear your thoughts?

CHAPTER 5

Forgiveness

Let's begin our lesson by opening our Bible to the Book Of *John* and <u>read</u> *Chapter 4 verses 1-42*.

St. John 4:1-42 will be the foundation that <u>Women on the R.U.N. for Jesus</u> is built on.

---

*Be kind to each other, sympathetic, **forgiving** each other as God has **forgiven** you through Christ.* (Ephesians 4:32)

First to begin with, I always start out by putting God first in everything I do and I will like to take this moment just to thank Him and call His name. Please pray along with me:

Heavenly Father, I thank you. I thank you for giving me the wisdom to reach out to the world. Lord, I give you the praise. I give you the glory. I give you the honor. I worship you O Lord, for you are Sovereign in my life. You are Alpha and Omega. Lord, I thank you for directing my steps and having mercy on me because I know that I am not perfect. I need you Father, in my life each and every day. I know there is always something in me that you are working on and I surrender all to you. I acknowledge Father, that I am not always pleasing to you, but because you are Wonderful, because you are Merciful, I know that your love is everlasting. I thank you Father for purifying my mind and using me in whatever way that is pleasing to you and forgive me Father for anything that is not pleasing to you. Lord, I thank you for allowing me to renew my mind each and every day so that I can hear more from you. I pray this prayer, in Jesus name. Amen.

Lord, I lift up every woman and their families in this class that I am about to teach in the Name of Jesus. Lord, I ask that they come to you with a clean heart, a loving heart, a forgiving heart. Lord, help them to keep the Focus on you Father. Touch their hearts Father. Lord you know each and everyone's needs. Healing for pain in the knee. Healing for foot ache. Healing for headache. Healing for their children, loved ones. Whatever the need is, Father. I come to you in agreement with each of these women today that all their needs will be met, in the Name of Jesus. Amen.

Do I have a witness today, if it wasn't for the Lord on your side, you would have (fill in). . . . . . for yelling at you. You would have (fill in). . . . . . for accusing you of (fill in). . . . . whatever the situation, you felt like someone did you wrong and you do not want to forgive that person. You were boiling up inside! But the devil is a liar! I come today to tell you that because you are in Christ, that whatever the situation, you are a forgiving person, *so therefore submit to God, resist the devil, and he will flee.* (James 4:7)

I had lunch with a former co-worker. As we sat down to eat, she asked me, "Can God forgive someone many times?" I said, "Yes" She asked me again, "Can God forgive someone who has a gambling problem and gambles over and over again?" I said, "Yes, God will forgive someone that has a gambling problem." She continued, "Can He forgive a person who gambles and will not stop gambling?" 'Yes, I said, *God is faithful and reliable. If we confess our sins, He forgives them and cleanses us from everything we've done wrong.* (1 John 1:9) She said, "She does not believe in God." I seized this opportunity to tell her that God forgives us if we come to Him and confess our sins. I sensed in my spirit that she was bitter and hurting. *(when you have a relationship, a true relationship with the Holy Spirit: He will reveal truth to you.)*

She was so confused because she is not a believer and does not understand.

John 3:16: *God loved the world this way: He gave his only Son so that everyone who believes in him will not die but will have eternal life.*

I knew she was hurting when she was telling her story. I wanted her to know Jesus like I know Jesus. I wanted her to believe in God.

I believe that it is not humanly possible to forgive someone who has deeply hurt you and those you love. Forgiveness is a process that we cannot understand. It is a gift from our Lord and Savior Jesus Christ. No doubt, there are a lot of us that will not agree with this statement. Forgiveness does not come naturally to us. We try to get even, but God encourages us to give and to love. God's love is stronger than us taking revenge.

Do you sometimes carry bitterness towards someone who has offended or hurt you?

The Bible says: *And when you stand praying, forgive anyone you have anything against. Then your Father in heaven will forgive your sins.* (Mark 11:26)

But for some it is easy to forgive; and it is not so easy for others. I remember I was very upset. I was hurt many times by those who wrongfully said words that hurt me. I had to forgive them. I know that Jesus does not want us to carry any wrong thought towards anyone. I use to retaliate and say hurtful words. I had to stop, repent and apologize to those whom I hurt. We expect the other person to apologize, but the Bible says: *Anyone you forgive I also forgive. Was there anything to forgive? If so, I have forgiven it for your benefit, knowing that Christ is watching.* (2 Corinthians 2:10)

Each of us is responsible for our actions. We should be careful when we speak. We need to forgive each other and have a clean heart towards each other. When you forgive, you have a calmer more relaxed and peaceful spirit. Do not hold onto any grudge towards anyone for you will be destroying yourself by having worrisome thoughts. God does not want us to have worrisome thoughts. And remember Christ is watching! God wants us to **Love** each other. **Respect** each other and **Forgive** each other.

Meditate:
Matthew 18:18-20

Pray:
I am inviting all "Women on the R.U.N. for Jesus" to spend a minimum of one (1) hour daily in prayer.

Read: Matthew 18:21-35

Do you believe it is humanly possible to forgive those who have deeply hurt you or someone you love? Why or why not?
What does Jesus say about forgiveness? Why should we forgive?

CHAPTER 6

Trusting God

Let's begin our lesson by opening our Bible to the Book Of *John* and <u>read</u> *Chapter 4 verses 1-42*.

St. John 4:1-42 will be the foundation that <u>Women on the R.U.N. for Jesus</u> is built on.

Going through a painful trial or heartache can bring you down lower than you have ever been. It can seem unbearable and crushing especially when you don't understand why God would allow this struggle in your life. How can the torment that you are experiencing be part of God's perfect plan for you? It just doesn't make sense.

The things that come against us in this world will never make sense to us. However, that does not mean that there is not a purpose for all that happens. In Luke 22:43-44 we read: *that Jesus went to the Mount of Olives to pray before He was to be crucified. With great anguish over what He was to suffer, His sweat was like drops of blood falling to the ground.*

Yet as He obeyed His Father's will, an angel from heaven appeared and strengthened Him. Jesus understood that there were eternal implications in all that He had to endure. He willingly gave His life that we might be saved.

As a believer, you should understand that God will also send His angels to strengthen and comfort you as you grow weary from the battles of this world. He will never let you stand alone and carry burdens that are much too heavy for you. The Lord knows how to rescue godly men from their trials. His purpose in allowing pain in your life is to develop you into the image of Christ and to actually make you stronger for the journey set before you. In 2 Corinthians 4:8-9, God's word says: *that you may be hard pressed on all sides but never crushed; perplexed, but not in despair; persecuted but never abandoned; struck down, but not destroyed.* The storms of this life can rock your boat but Jesus has promised that you will get to the destination that He planned for you before you were born. When you can trust God despite your broken heart, you defeat the father of lies who wants you to forget that Jesus paid the price for your victory. All the troubles that we must face are obtaining for us an eternal reward that will last forever. You must keep your eyes on Jesus who is able to keep you in 'perfect peace' even when you don't understand the purpose for your pain.

Scripture says that after losing his children, his wealth and his health, Job cried out, *"Though He slay me, yet will I trust Him"* (Job 13:15). God had a purpose in allowing Job to go through such a trial. Ultimately, Satan was defeated and Job received a great reward. He was given beautiful children, greater wealth and a longer life because he trusted God even when all was taken.

God's purpose and plan will forever stand though the earth may be shaken. God's ways are much higher than the logic of this world so you must trust Him even when you don't understand. There is nothing you are suffering that God didn't plan in advance to take you through. May it help you to know that there are believers praying for you right now and that God's love for you will never fail!

There was a time in my life when I was trusting God for many things, saying God, I want this and I want that, then the Lord showed me it's not all about what I want but to just trust Him. Some of us ask God for many materialistic things and when it does not happen the way we would like, we get disappointed. We need to trust God in all situations, good and bad.

God does not always deliver us from everything when we think He should. Throughout His Word, we read about people who had to go *through* things.

One familiar passage to many people is Psalm 23:4, "*Yes, though I walk through the [deep, sunless] valley of the shadow of death, I will fear or dread no evil, for You are with me*" (*The Amplified Bible*). Psalm 66:12 says, "*You caused men to ride over our heads [when we were prostrate]; we went through fire and through water, but You brought us out into a broad, moist place [to abundance and refreshment and the open air].*"

And the prophet Isaiah, speaking for God, says: "*When you pass through the waters, I will be with you, and through the rivers, they will not overwhelm you. When you walk through the fire, you will not be burned or scorched, nor will the flame kindle upon you*" (Is. 43:2, emphasis added).

Every problem and troubling situation believer's face in this life is allowed by God for a specific purpose. He is working out something far greater than what appears to be happening as He guides the process of transforming you into the image of Christ. Your faith is being sharpened as a sword to equip you for the battles of this world. The path of victory has already been set and there is nothing that can destroy a believer who has put his faith in the cross of Jesus. We are commanded to be anxious for nothing and no one. But, is that still possible when the darkness of the storm surrounds us?

The truth is that the strength to endure every painful trial is with you in Christ. If your eyes were opened to view the spiritual battle that is raging, you would see the grand army of the living God totally surrounding and protecting you with powerful weapons far greater than those against you. Though you will still endure the attacks of the enemy, your hope of victory is secure because of the cross of Christ. You may be feeling weary and completely overwhelmed but the Bible tells us that God is close to the broken-hearted and He is near to us in our pain. He does not abandon you when your situation is bleak. As you lift up your fears to Him in thankfulness and prayer, you allow His power to be unleashed in your life as He takes your struggle and makes it work into His perfect plan for you. God knows your weaknesses and has seen your failures yet His power is more than enough to take you safely through. You may be wounded but you will never be destroyed!

The Bible says this about trusting God, *"Trust in the LORD with all your heart and lean not on your own understanding"* (Proverbs 3:5). Furthermore, it tells us that "he *who trusts in himself is a fool . . ."* (Proverbs 28:26). Still, most of us have difficulty trusting God at least at one point or another in our walk with Him. There are probably many reasons why trusting is difficult. God's ways don't always make sense to us. God told Noah to build an ark. It may have never rained up to this point and the nearest body of water was probably many miles away. It could not have made much sense to Noah at all *(story found in Genesis 6-8)*. We want life to make sense. We always want to set our own terms and timetables. Are you trusting in God in times of difficulties?

Meditate:
Matthew 18:18-20

Pray:
I am inviting all "Women on the R.U.N. for Jesus" to spend a minimum of one (1) hour daily in prayer.

Read: 2 Corinthians Chapter 4

CHAPTER 7

Meditation

Let's begin our lesson by opening our Bible to the Book Of *John* and <u>read</u> *Chapter 4 verses 1-42*.

St. John 4:1-42 will be the foundation that <u>Women on the R.U.N. for Jesus</u> is built on.

I would like you to meditate for a few minutes on the Lord and all that He has done for you today. Slowly begin to listen to that still small Voice speaking on the inside of you. Feel yourself slowly becoming one with the Creator of the Universe. Now completely let go and let your Daddy God minister to those areas of your life that you have been keeping from Him. Release and experience increase as the Holy Spirit fills those empty places in your hurting heart.

As I stated in my book, "Telling It All From The Heart" (Authorhouse) Meditation has been and will continue to be a great relaxing process in my life. I love to meditate and I love to pray. This brings such a calmness to my body, my spirit and to my soul. Everyone should learn to meditate, and everyone should develop a prayer life. Meditation should be a part of our everyday life. Without meditation and prayer, I believe I would be missing an important part of my daily routine, meditating and prayer. I put all my trust in my Daddy God to come into my body, my spirit and my soul and guide me throughout the day when I meditate. This process begins when I thank my Savior for being in my life and also in my loved ones lives'. When I meditate, it relaxes my body and when I pray it brings peace to my soul and also upon my fellow brothers and sisters around me. Having a calm and peaceful spirit within myself is very important to God, because it allows Him to fill me as I seek God more and to hear from Him. (pg. 52)

Rick Warren, in *The Purpose Driven Life* (Zondervan), describes meditation this way: "Meditation is *focused* thinking. It takes serious effort. You select a verse and reflect on it over and over in your mind . . . if you know how to worry, you already know how to meditate" (pg.190). Warren goes on to say, "No other habit can do more to transform your life and make you more like Jesus than daily reflection on Scripture . . . If you look up all the times God speaks about meditation in the Bible, you will amazed at the benefits He has promised to those who take the time to reflect on His Word throughout the day" (pg.190).

In *Satisfy Your Soul* (NavPress), Dr. Bruce Demarest writes, "A quieted heart is our best preparation for all this work of God . . . Meditation refocuses us from ourselves and from the world so that we reflect on God's Word, His nature, His abilities, and His works . . . So we prayerfully ponder, muse, and 'chew' the words of Scripture . . . . The goal is simply to permit the Holy Spirit to activate the life-giving Word of God" (pg.133).

When you meditate, you step outside the dry landscape of everyday life, into the warm shower of blessings God has provided for you, opening your heart to the spiritual refreshment of intimacy with Him.

In meditation, God deepens your relationship with Him. And as you rest in that relationship, He works His love into your heart, drawing you deeper and nearer to Him.

Meditation allows the nourishing richness of God's love to flow into the deep places of your heart and spirit, soul and body. The depth of His love flows into the depth of your pain and need . . . healing you, and transforming you.

Perhaps most reassuring of all is knowing that He does the work. You open your heart, and let His love wash through you. Tightly held hurts begin to open, spaces clear, knots unravel, hard places soften . . . and as His light shines in, your heart becomes a more true place, and you are more able to be His person in the world. You become more and more the person you were always created to be.

————————————————

Meditate:
Matthew 18:18-20

Pray:
I am inviting all "Women on the R.U.N. for Jesus" to spend a minimum of one (1) hour daily in prayer.

Read: Psalm 119:97-99

What has meditation done for you?
Do you meditate on God's word daily?
Have you practiced meditation and allow the Holy Spirit to come into your heart and speak to you?

CHAPTER 8

God's Voice

Let's begin our lesson by opening our Bible to the Book Of *John* and <u>read</u> *Chapter 4 verses 1-42*.

St. John 4:1-42 will be the foundation that <u>Women on the R.U.N. for Jesus</u> is built on.

First to begin with, I always start out by putting God first in everything I do and I will like to take this moment just to thank Him and call His name. Please pray along with me:

Heavenly Father, I thank you. I thank you for giving me the wisdom to reach out to the world. Lord, I give you the praise. I give you the glory. I give you the honor. I worship you O Lord, for you are Sovereign in my life. You are Alpha and Omega. Lord, I thank you for directing my steps and having mercy on me because I know that I am not perfect. I need you Father, in my life each and every day. I know there is always something in me that you are working on and I surrender all to you. I acknowledge Father, that I am not always pleasing to you, but because you are Wonderful, because you are Merciful, I know that your love is everlasting. I thank you Father for purifying my mind and using me in whatever way that is pleasing to you and forgive me Father for anything that is not pleasing to you. Lord, I thank you for allowing me to renew my mind each and every day so that I can hear more from you. I pray this prayer, in Jesus name. Amen.

Lord, I lift up every woman and their families in this class that I am about to teach in the Name of Jesus. Lord, I ask that they come to you with a clean heart, a loving heart, a forgiving heart. Lord, help them to keep the Focus on you Father. Touch their hearts Father. Lord you know each and everyone's needs. Healing for pain in the knee. Healing for foot ache. Healing for headache. Healing for their children, loved ones. Whatever the need is, Father. I come to you in agreement with each of these women today that all their needs will be met, in the Name of Jesus. Amen.

When Rhoda recognized Peter's voice, because of her gladness she did not open the gate, but ran in and announced that Peter stood before the gate. (Acts 12:14) Rhoda never saw Peter. Instead, she shared by faith that it was Peter because she knew the sound of his voice. How do we respond when the Lord speaks to us?

Do we respond by faith or respond by fear?

How do you respond when the Lord speaks to you?

This is a Question most Christians ask.

These questions are sometimes not so easily answered.

In order to hear from God we must be Obedient,

Loving, and attentive to God's Word:

We Must Wait Upon The Lord.

Psalm 40:1 "I waited patiently for the Lord; and He inclined to me, and heard my cry."

We sometimes get impatient when the answer to prayer takes longer than we expect. Being patient is important in order to hear from the Holy Spirit. By reading the Bible, by asking God, by seeking His will, we can know what His will is in many cases. In some instances where the Bible is not specific and we ask God something about life's direction, who to marry, what job to take, etc., we must wait in order to hear from the Holy Spirit.

We can discern the will of the Holy Spirit by becoming aware of an increase or decrease of desire in our hearts as we repeatedly pray and wait on Him. In other words, God often puts a desire into our hearts that increases over time as we pray about something if it is in agreement with scripture, then it is most probably from the Lord. If the desire in your heart decreases it may be that the Lord is not speaking to you on that topic. Look at it this way. Pray and ask the Lord to increase desires in your heart that are from Him, and decrease those that are not. And, always make sure your desires are in accordance with the Bible.

We Must Confess Our Sins

Psalm 66:18, "If I regard iniquity in my heart, The Lord will not hear."

If there are sins in your life from which you have not turned, then you need to confess them before the Lord and be cleansed.

We Must Be Still

Psalm 46:10 encourages us to be still, and know that He is God.

We Must Stand Before Him

1 King 19:11-13 When you become still. You are able to hear that quiet, still voice of God, but when you are not still you hear your own inner thoughts. Then He said, "Go out, and stand on the mountain before the LORD." And behold, the LORD passed by, and a great and strong wind tore into the mountains and broke the rocks in pieces before the LORD, *but* the LORD *was* not in the wind; and after the wind an earthquake, *but* the LORD *was* not in the earthquake; and after the earthquake a fire, *but* the LORD *was* not in the fire; and after the fire a **still small voice**. So it was, when Elijah heard *it,* that he wrapped his face in his mantle and went out and stood in the entrance of the cave. Suddenly a voice *came* to him, and said, "What are you doing here, Elijah?"

Meditate:
Matthew 18:18-20

Pray:
I am inviting all "Women on the R.U.N. for Jesus" to spend a minimum of one (1) hour daily in prayer.

Read: Romans 10:17

CHAPTER 9

Praising God

Let's begin our lesson by opening our Bible to the Book Of *John* and <u>read</u> *Chapter 4 verses 1-42*.

St. John 4:1-42 will be the foundation that <u>Women on the R.U.N. for Jesus</u> is built on.

Praising Him

How wonderful it is to be in God's Presence. **Psalm 34:1** says we should bless the Lord at all times, His praise shall be continuously be in our mouth. I love to praise God. I am always on fire for God. I get in His Presence and start praising Him. Giving Him thanks and Blessing His Holy Name. God is good and He is good all the time. When we have tribulations, God is good. Early in the morning, God is good. I rise early in the morning, and I encourage you to rise early too and thank God for another day. Lifting up Holy hands and exalting His Holy name.

Here what the Bible says In Psalm 47:

Praise to God, the Ruler of the Earth

Oh, clap your hands, all you peoples! Shout to God with the voice of triumph! For the LORD Most High *is* awesome; *He is* a great King over all the earth. He will subdue the peoples under us, And the nations under our feet. He will choose our inheritance for us, The excellence of Jacob whom He loves. Selah

God has gone up with a shout, The LORD with the sound of a trumpet. Sing praises to God, sing praises! Sing praises to our King, sing praises! For God *is* the King of all the earth; Sing praises with understanding.

God reigns over the nations; God sits on His holy throne. The princes of the people have gathered together, The people of the God of Abraham. For the shields of the earth *belong* to God; He is greatly exalted.

Isn't it wonderful to praise God? I will rejoice and be glad in Him. I will listen to the timbrel and dance. I will sing and clap my hands. I will lift up my hands to Him, my God, my Savior. I will cry out to Him. I will kneel at His feet. I will read His Word. I will have a conversation with Him. I will always have an intimate relationship with Him for He is such a good God. He is a Merciful God. He is a Forgiving God. He is a Loving God. He is a Wonderful God. He is a Marvelous God. He is a God who never changes. He is a God who never leaves you nor forsake you. He is I Am that I Am. He is a Delivering God. I can go on and on. Thank you Jesus. I will never stop Praising Your Name.

Praise God (from Whom all Blessings Flow) written by Thomas Ken:

Praise God, from Whom all blessings flow; Praise Him, all creatures here below; Praise Him above, ye heavenly host; Praise Father, Son, and Holy Ghost.

Sing this song and enjoy the presence of God within.

Song and Praises to the Lord

I Surrender All *J.W. Van Deventer / W.S. Weeden*

All to Jesus I surrender,
All to Him I freely give;

I will ever love and trust Him,
In His presence daily live.

I surrender all,
I surrender all.
All to Thee, my blessed Savior,
I surrender all.

All to Jesus I surrender,
Humbly at His feet I bow,
Worldly pleasures all forsaken;
Take me, Jesus, take me now.

All to Jesus I surrender,
Make me, Savior, wholly Thine;
Let me feel Thy Holy Spirit,
Truly know that Thou art mine.

All to Jesus I surrender,
Lord, I give myself to Thee;
Fill me with Thy love and power,
Let Thy blessing fall on me.

All to Jesus I surrender,
Now I feel the sacred flame.

Oh, the joy of full salvation!
Glory, glory to His name!

Surrender All to Jesus. When we surrender all to Him, we make Him our First in everything and allow Him to work in our Lives. Just leave everything in His care.

Why We Should Praise God

Praising God is important because He is worthy to be praised. Let me share a testimony with you.

"On Friday, January 4, 2013", I was filled with the Holy Spirit. I told my husband, please put the CD on with the song, "*Something Happens*", by Preashea Hilliard. I played that song until the Holy Spirit told me to turn it off which was early Saturday Morning. I knew the Holy Spirit was going to use me but I did not know how. On Sunday, my husband and I went to morning service, As we entered the Sanctuary we were seated by the ushers. The words to the song "*Something Happens*" began to play and immediately entered into my Spirit. I knew the Holy Spirit was doing something. I felt a glow of heat inside of me and all I knew the Holy Spirit was leading me to tell His people, "There's something about that Name called Jesus and what Happens when we call His Name. Hallelujah Jesus. Praise His Name.

By praising God, we are reminded of the greatness of God! His power and presence in our lives is reinforced in our understanding. "Praise the Lord, for the Lord is good; sing praises to His name, for it is pleasant" (Psalm 135:3).

I will extol the LORD at all times; His praise shall continually be in my mouth (Psalm 34:1)."

- *"Because Your loving kindness is better than life, My lips shall praise you. Thus I will Bless You while I live; I will lift up my hands in Your name." (Psalm 63:3-4).*
- *"Behold, Bless the LORD, all you servants of the LORD who by night stand in the house of the LORD. Lift up your hands in the sanctuary and Bless the LORD" (Psalm 134:1-2).*

Psalm 150:1-6

Praise the LORD!

Praise God in His sanctuary; Praise Him in His mighty firmament!

Praise Him for His mighty acts; Praise Him according to His excellent greatness!

Praise Him with the sound of the trumpet; Praise Him with the lute and harp! Praise Him with the timbrel and dance; Praise Him with stringed instruments and flutes! Praise Him with loud cymbals; Praise Him with clashing cymbals!

Let everything that has breath praise the LORD.

Praise the LORD!

Psalm 95:1-11

Oh come, let us sing to the LORD! Let us shout joyfully to the Rock of our salvation. Let us come before His presence with thanksgiving; Let us shout joyfully to Him with psalms. For the LORD *is* the great God, And the great King above all gods. In His hand *are* the deep places of the earth; The heights of the hills *are* His also. The sea *is* His, for He made it; And His hands formed the dry *land.*

Oh come, let us worship and bow down; Let us kneel before the LORD our Maker. For He *is* our God, And we *are* the people of His pasture, And the sheep of His hand.

Today, if you will hear His voice: Do not harden your hearts, as in the rebellion, As *in* the day of trial in the wilderness, When your fathers tested Me; They tried Me, though they saw My work. For forty years I was grieved with *that* generation, And said, 'It *is* a people who go astray in their hearts, And they do not know My ways.' So I swore in My wrath, They shall not enter My rest.

Meditate:
Matthew 18:18-20

Pray:
I am inviting all "Women on the R.U.N. for Jesus" to spend a minimum of one (1) hour daily in prayer.

Read: Psalm 150:1-6

What Does the Bible Say About Praising God?
How many times a day do you Praise God?
Meditate on the Scripture verses on Praising God.
Apply it to your life daily.

CHAPTER 10

Friends

Let's begin our lesson by opening our Bible to the Book Of *John* and <u>read</u> *Chapter 4 verses 1-42*.

St. John 4:1-42 will be the foundation that <u>Women on the R.U.N. for Jesus </u> is built on.

CONNECTING WITH THE RIGHT ONES

Father, I thank you once again for giving me the wisdom to reach out to souls that have a desire to serve you. Please pray with me:

Lord, we love you, we ask you Father, in Jesus Name to watch over our children, our loved ones, our friends, our household, the leaders of each country. Lord, as we renew our minds, help us to stay focused on your Word, and not on the materialistic things of this world. Lord, we lift you higher, each and every day. We love you Father, We adore you. We thank you. We worship you. We give you all the glory, in Jesus Precious Name . . . . Amen

---

Let me start out by saying:

Connecting with right people is very important. Not everyone can be your friend. People who are with you are not always for you. A man *who has* friends must himself be friendly, but there is a friend *who* sticks closer than a brother. (Proverbs 18:24)

We live in a society where we are all different in our own way. We all have a role to play in our lives. There is good, and there is bad in us, but we all have different personalities. We should be treated with love, but it does not always work that way. We should not do things for others if we are not doing it out of love. Society is so selfish. We should love one another and not criticize each other. I sometimes wonder why we could be so selfish, so caught up in ourselves that others' opinion does not always matter or soothe our thinking. We may not see the negative part in ourselves but others will. I know when I am negative, I can feel it when I speak sometimes, but then I become positive in not letting my negative side overpower me. *("Telling It All From The Heart" p18)*

When I wrote my self-published book, it was not about money. It was all about helping hurting people. It was all about "Telling It All From The Heart" and how God gave me favor. How He brought me out of some trials and tribulations. I was not sure how God was going to use me, but I thank God for using me mightily.

I had a woman tell me how she prayed the prayers from my book and it touched her so much, she felt the presence of God moving in her. *("Telling It All From The Heart" p68)*

I had a woman who told me that she could not forgive and by reading on forgiveness, she was able to forgive. *("Telling It All From The Heart" p30)*

I have received many testimonies from people that were touched by reading passages in my book.

It is amazing how God blessed me and worked in my life all because He give me favor in stepping out in Faith.

Money, Money, Money. People emphasize on money, but is God a part of what they are doing? *No one can **serve** two masters. Either he will hate the one and love the other, or he will be devoted to the one and despise the other. You cannot **serve** both **God** and **Money**.* (Matthew 6:24) Are they reaching out to help others?

What did God call you to do?

How can we recognize potential friendship? Signs include a mutual desire for companionship and perhaps a common bond of some kind. Beyond that, genuine friendship involves a shared sense of caring and concern, a desire to see one another grow and develop, and a hope for each other to succeed in all aspects of life. True friendship involves action: doing something for someone else while expecting nothing in return; sharing thoughts and feelings without fear of judgment or negative criticism.

After Arthur and I were married, I tried to stay connected to my friends but for some reason the connection and phone calls became less frequent. It seemed that I was always the one making the calls and trying to keep the connection but the few I thought were my friends acted very negatively when the question was asked, "I am not hearing from you anymore?" The reply was, "You're married!" I realized that God was separating me from these people. God was taking me to another season.

When Arthur and I were planning our wedding; we were not connected to the right people. But in the end God brought the right people to plan our wedding. God worked everything out fine because He was our Wedding Planner. God will always connect you with the right people.

A true friend is not jealous.
A true friend is giving.
A true friend will not turn their backs on you.
A true friend is there for you, in times of struggle.
A true friend does not gossip about you.
A true friend will support you.

Do I have a witness in the house who knows what I am saying?

A true friend will encourage you to go higher.
A true friend will not discourage you from what you are doing for the Lord.
A true friend will not talk you out of your dreams.

A true friend makes no excuses of having work or appointments or anything but will be with you whenever you need him/her. In your hour of desperation, a true friend will support you even if the whole world opposes you.

HOW MANY OF US HAVE TRUE FRIENDS? DO I HAVE A WITNESS?

You see, my friends, I have one true friend and His name is Jesus. I can call Him every night and He will be right there to listen. I can cry to Him when I feel the need and He will be there to dry my tears. I can ask Him to heal me and He will heal me. I can ask Him for strength when I am weak and He will give me strength. I can talk to Him anytime and He will always be there to listen. I ask Him everyday to watch over my children, my husband and I know He will be protecting them. That's a true friend. Whenever, I need my friend, I know He will never leave me nor forsake me because I've learned to trust in my friend Jesus, because He never failed me yet. *Abraham believed **God**, and it was credited to him as righteousness," and he was called **God's friend**.* (James 2:23) And like faithful Abraham we can call God friend too.

A true friend is not an opportunist. Instead of having hundreds of good friends, if you have a true friend, you are blessed. If you can also become a true friend to someone, you will be blessed, because it is much easier for all of us to accept but very difficult to give. Be a true friend yourself first.

Proverbs 18:19 in the New Living Translation says: *It's harder to make amends with an offended friend than to capture a fortified city.* Arguments separate friends like a gate locked with iron bars. When we've offended a true friend - whether by breaking a trust or by speaking the truth with love - we risk losing that friendship. We must be careful not to break the trust. But when not speaking the truth will cause greater hurt in our friend's life, **we must be willing to sacrifice our needs for those of our friend. That is true friendship.**

Not many of us have true friends. But know for certain, you have a true friend and His name is Jesus. DO I HAVE A WITNESS . . . . . . ?

———————————————

Meditate:
Matthew 18:18-20

Pray:
I am inviting all "Women on the R.U.N. for Jesus" to spend a minimum of one (1) hour daily in prayer.

Read: John 15:13-16

CHAPTER 11

Faith

Let's begin our lesson by opening our Bible to the Book Of *John* and <u>read</u> *Chapter 4 verses 1-42.*

St. John 4:1-42 will be the foundation that <u>Women on the R.U.N. for Jesus</u> is built on.

Let's talk about Faith. Having Faith in God is so very important in our lives. Without Faith it is impossible to please God. There are times when we pray about a need or something of effect and we have doubt, fear about whether we will hear from God. We want things to happen tomorrow. When what we ask God for does not come when we want it, we begin to get discouraged. God does not do things in our time. He does things in His time. God does things beautifully in His time. Waiting on God is the best. When we give our request to God we should leave all our cares in His hand. God will never leave us nor forsake us. He knows what is best for us. We need to keep holding on to God's hand.

What is Faith?

Now faith is the substance of things hoped for, the evidence of things not seen. Hebrews 11:1

**We are going to touch on two (2) types of Faith:
Healing Faith and Saving Faith**

Here are some Scripture verses about people who were healed because of their Faith:

Now a certain woman had a flow of blood for twelve years, and had suffered many things from many physicians. She had spent all that she had and was no better, but rather grew worse. When she heard about Jesus, she came behind *Him* in the crowd and touched His garment. For she said, "If only I may touch His clothes, I shall be made well." Immediately the fountain of her blood was dried up, and she felt in *her* body that she was healed of the affliction. And Jesus, immediately knowing in Himself that power had gone out of Him, turned around in the crowd and said, "Who touched My clothes?" But His disciples said to Him, "You see the multitude thronging You, and You say, 'Who touched Me?'" And He looked around to see her who had done this thing. But the woman, fearing and trembling, knowing what had happened to her, came and fell down before Him and told Him the whole truth. And He said to her, "Daughter, your faith has made you well. Go in peace, and be healed of your affliction." **Mark 5:25-34**

Then Jesus went out from there and departed to the region of Tyre and Sidon. And behold, a woman of Canaan came from that region and cried out to Him, saying, "Have mercy on me, O Lord, Son of David! My daughter is severely demon-possessed." But He answered her not a word. And His disciples came and urged Him, saying. "Send her away, for she cries out after us." But He answered and said, 'I was not sent except to the lost sheep of the house of Israel." Then she came and worshipped Him, saying,

"Lord, help me!" But He answered and said, "It is not good to take the children's bread and throw it to the little dogs." And she said, "Yes, Lord, yet even the little dogs eat the crumbs which fall from their masters' table." Then Jesus answered and said to her, O woman, great is your faith! Let it be to you as you desire." And her daughter was healed from that very hour. **Matthew 15:21-28**

Now in the morning, as He returned to the city, He was hungry. And seeing a fig tree by the road, He came to it and found nothing on it but leaves, and said to it. "Let no fruit grow on you ever again." Immediately the fig tree withered away. And when the disciples saw it, they marveled, saying. "How did the fig tree wither away so soon?" And Jesus answered them, "Assuredly, I say to you, if you have faith and do not doubt, you will not only do what was done to the fig tree, but also if you say to this mountain, 'Be removed and be cast into the sea,' it will be done. [22] And whatever things you ask in prayer, believing, you will receive." **Matthew 21:21-22**

And Jesus said to him, "Go your way; your faith has made you well." And immediately he received his sight and followed Jesus on the road. **Mark 10:52**

Here is some scriptures about people who were saved because of their faith:

So God, who knows the heart, acknowledged them by giving them the Holy Spirit, just as *He did* to us, and made no distinction between us and them, purifying their hearts by faith. **Acts 15:8-9**

And when they had come to him, he said to them: "You know, from the first day that I came to Asia, in what manner I always lived among you, serving the Lord with all humility, with many tears and trials which happened to me by the plotting of the Jews; how I kept back nothing that was helpful, but proclaimed it to you, and taught you publicly and from house to house, testifying to Jews, and also to Greeks, repentance toward God and faith toward our Lord Jesus Christ. **Acts 20:18-21**

For I am not ashamed of the gospel, for it is the power of God for salvation to everyone who believes, to the Jew first and also to the Greek. For in it the righteousness of God is revealed from faith for faith, as it is written, "The righteous shall live by faith." **Romans 1:16-17**

And since we have the same spirit of faith according to what is written, "I believed, and therefore I spoke," we also believe, and therefore speak, knowing that He who raised up the Lord Jesus will also raise us up with Jesus, and will present us with you. **2 Corinthians 4:13-14**

_____

Meditate:
Matthew 18:18-20

Pray:
I am inviting all "Women on the R.U.N. for Jesus" to spend a minimum of one (1) hour daily in prayer.

Read: Hebrews Chapter 11

CHAPTER 12

Encouragement

Let's begin our lesson by opening our Bible to the Book Of *John* and <u>read</u> *Chapter 4 verses 1-42.*

St. John 4:1-42 will be the foundation that <u>Women on the R.U.N. for Jesus </u> is built on.

You cannot force someone to like you. If a person does not like you, no matter what you do, that person still will not like you. Some people are selfish, some people are rude, some people are just plain anti-social. We serve a God of Love. Jesus is Love. When a person rejects you, they are rejecting Christ. The Bible tells us to hate sin but love the sinner. We need Godly direction in order to encourage others. There were times in my life, when I was afraid to call certain people because I did not know how they would receive me. We must have the love of God within us always even though others may treat us harshly.

Let's Get Real With God

Let's get real with God. Let's stop the bitterness and strife between each other. Let's put away childish behavior. Let's spend time with God and get into His Word and Let His Word come alive in our hearts. God is calling. We must listen to His voice and ask for His Grace and Mercy when it comes to dealing with others.

Let's begin to walk with God. Talk with God. Praise Him in the morning and Praise Him until the sun goes down. Let's encourage one another and not gossip amongst each other. We are not perfect but we can ask God to change us. He can deliver you from your sinful lifestyle. Just believe and trust Him. God is Real. I repeat. God is Real. Earlier, I said that God does not make JUNK. Every good thing comes from God. We are God's children. Let's show Him how much He means to us.

Let's put away gossip, anger, hatred, whatever you are struggling with and give it to God. Let's take it to Him and drop it in His lap. Surrender all to Jesus. Forget about yourselves and worship Him and give Him thanks.

Thank you Father for delivering us, cleansing our spirit, soul and body. Remove everything in us that is not like you. Break stuff off Father. Shift some stuff Father. O Lord. Thank you for all what you are doing so we can follow your steps. Have your way Lord, Have your way!

We hear the word Encouragement many times. Do we encourage others? Some of us may say sometimes, some may say very rarely or some may say no. When we encourage each other, we know that God is pleased. Sometimes we do not know what a person may be going through, that's why it is very important to encourage one another. Speaking a kind loving word to someone may brighten his/her day. It may be just the Good News that they were waiting to hear.

If you feel forgotten or abandoned by God, give yourself a praise talk.

Remind yourself about God's goodness and how His promises are true. Spend time in His Word, looking up and memorizing one Scripture that will motivate you toward a personal revelation of faith.

Verses to Read For Encouragement:
Psalm 83:1 Do not keep silent, O God! Do not hold Your peace, And do not be still, O God!

Jeremiah 29:13-14 And you will seek Me and find *Me,* when you search for Me with all your heart. I will be found by you, says the LORD, and I will bring you back from your captivity; I will gather you from all the nations and from all the places where I have driven you, says the LORD, and I will bring you to the place from which I cause you to be carried away captive.

Proverbs 24:20 For there will be no prospect for the evil *man;* The lamp of the wicked will be put out.

Proverbs 24:14 So *shall* the knowledge of wisdom *be* to your soul; If you have found *it,* there is a prospect, And your hope will not be cut off.

Jeremiah 29:11 For I know the thoughts that I think toward you, says the LORD, thoughts of peace and not of evil, to give you a future and a hope.

Titus 1:1-2 Paul, a bondservant of God and an apostle of Jesus Christ, according to the faith of God's elect and the acknowledgment of the truth which accords with godliness, in hope of eternal life which God, who cannot lie, promised before time began.

Titus 3:7 that having been justified by His grace we should become heirs according to the hope of eternal life.

1 Corinthians 15:19 If in this life only we have hope in Christ, we are of all men the most pitiable.

2 Corinthians 4:16-18 Therefore we do not lose heart. Even though our outward *man* is perishing, yet the inward man is being renewed day by day. For our light affliction, which is but for a moment, is working for us a far more exceeding *and* eternal weight of glory, while we do not look at the things which are seen, but at the things which are not seen. For the things which are seen *are* temporary, but the things which *are* not seen are eternal.

1 Peter 1:3 Blessed *be* the God and Father of our Lord Jesus Christ, who according to His abundant mercy has begotten us again to a living hope through the resurrection of Jesus Christ from the dead.

_____

Meditate:
Matthew 18:18-20

Pray:
I am inviting all "Women on The R.U.N. for Jesus" to spend a minimum of one (1) hour daily in prayer.

Read: Jeremiah 29:11-13

CHAPTER 13

Love

Let's begin our lesson by opening our Bible to the Book Of *John* and <u>read</u> *Chapter 4 verses 1-42*.

St. John 4:1-42 will be the foundation that <u>Women on the R.U.N. for Jesus </u> is built on.

Love is a very strong word. In order to love each other, you must first love yourself. If you do not love yourself, you will not be able to love another. You see, God loves each and every one of us unconditionally. When we give Love, we receive Love. If you do not give Love, you will not receive Love.

The Bible says we are to love one another. You see, God is love. Some of us are so unkind and disrespectful towards others because we do not practice the love of Jesus. Jesus suffered for us. He shed His blood. He was kicked, beaten, spat on, nailed to the cross. He was persecuted. Love died for us. Some of us do not know what true love is. We are so caught up within ourselves that we mistreat others because we are hurt. You see hurting people hurt people. Do I have a witness?

The Bible says:

1 Corinthians 13:4-13 *Love suffers long and is kind; love does not envy, love does not parade itself, is not puffed up; does not behave rudely, does not seek its own, is not provoked, thinks no evil; does not rejoice in iniquity, but rejoices in the truth; bears all things, believes all things, hopes all things, endures all things. Love never fails. But whether there are prophecies, they will fail; whether there are tongues, they will cease; whether there is knowledge, it will vanish away. For we know in part and we prophesy in part. But when that which is perfect has come, then that which is in part will be done away.*

When I was a child, I spoke as a child, I understand as a child, I thought as a child; but when I became a man, I put away childish things. For now we see in a mirror, dimly, but then face to face. Now I know in part, but then I shall know just as I also am know. And now abide faith, hope, love, these three; but the greatest of these is love.

John 3:16 *"For God so loved the world, that He gave His only Begotten Son, that whoever believes in Him should not perish but have everlasting life.*

Romans 5:8 *but God demonstrates His own love toward us, in that while we were still sinners, Christ died for us.*

Romans 8:37-39 *Yet in all these things we are more than conquerors through Him who loved us. For I am persuaded that neither death nor life, nor angels nor principalities, nor powers, nor things present, nor things to come, nor height nor depth, nor any other created thing, shall be able to separate us from the love of God which is in Christ Jesus our Lord.*

Galatians 2:20 *I have been crucified with Christ; it is no longer I who live, but Christ lives in me; and the life which I now live in the flesh I live by faith in the Son of God, who loved me and gave Himself for me.*

1 John 3:1 *Behold* what manner *of love the Father has bestowed on us, that we should be called children of God; therefore the world does not know us, because it did not know Him.*

Romans 13:8 *Owe no one anything except to love one another, he who loves another has fulfilled the law.*

Galatians 5:13 *For you, brethren, have been called to liberty; only do not use liberty as an opportunity for the flesh, but through love serve one another.*

Ephesians 4:2 *with all lowliness and gentleness, with long suffering, bearing with one another in love.*

1 Peter 1:22 *Since* you h*ave purified your souls in obeying the truth through the Spirit in sincere love of the brethren, love one another fervently with a pure heart.*

1 John 4:7 *Beloved, let us love one another, for love is of God; and everyone who loves is born of God and knows God.*

Matthew 5:43-48 "You have heard that it was said, 'You shall love your neighbor and hate your enemy.' But I say to you, love your enemies, bless those who curse you, do good to those who hate you, and pray for those who spitefully use you and persecute you, that you may be sons of your Father in heaven; for He makes His sun rise on the evil and on the good, and sends rain on the just and on the unjust. For if you love those who love you, what reward have you? Do not even the tax collectors do the same? And if you greet your brethren only, what do you do more *than others?* Do not even the tax collectors do so? Therefore you shall be perfect, just as your Father in heaven is perfect.

Matthew 6:24-25 "No one can serve two masters; for either he will hate the one and love the other, or else he will be loyal to the one and despise the other. You cannot serve God and mammon.

_____

Meditate:
Matthew 18:18-20

Pray:
I am inviting all "Women on the R.U.N. for Jesus" to spend a minimum of one (1) hour daily in prayer.

Read: 1 Corinthians Chapter 13
How do you apply Love in your life?

CHAPTER 14

Contentment and Strength

Let's begin our lesson by opening our Bible to the Book Of *John* and <u>read</u> *Chapter 4 verses 1-42.*

St. John 4:1-42 will be the foundation that <u>Women on the R.U.N. for Jesus</u> is built on.

Contentment is being satisfied with what we have. Not wanting more. There are some of us who are not content with what we have. We want a bigger house. We want a newer version of a car. We want more of what we really do not need. I have learned not to live like the Joneses' and look at my situation and to be satisfied with what God has given me. You see, **Philippians 4:19 tells me . . . . And my God will supply all your need according to his riches in glory by Christ Jesus.** Amen.

It is so good to know that we can rest in the strength and comfort that the Lord has provided when facing troubles of many kinds. Let God be the glory and show himself mighty. You see, **2Chronicles 16:9** *tells* me . . . . . **For the eyes of the LORD run to and fro throughout the whole earth, to show Himself strong on behalf of those whose heart is loyal to Him. In this you have done foolishly; therefore from now on you shall have wars."** Amen. God wants to show Himself strong on your behalf. Surrender to Him today and let the perfect peace that He already gave you take over. We cannot fully serve God without our contentment and His Strength.

Philippians 4:10-12. *But I rejoiced in the Lord greatly that now at last your care for me has flourished again; though you surely did care, but you lacked opportunity. Not that I speak in regard to need, for I have learned in whatever state I am, to be content I know how to be abased, and I know how to abound. Everywhere and in all things I have learned both to be full and to be hungry, both to abound and to suffer need.*

Isaiah 40:28-31 *Have you not known? Have you not heard? The everlasting God, the LORD, The Creator of the ends of the earth, Neither faints nor is weary. His understanding is unsearchable. He gives power to the weak, And to those who have no might He increases strength. Even the youths shall faint and be weary, And the young men shall utterly fall, But those who wait on the LORD Shall renew their strength; They shall mount up with wings like eagles, They shall run and not be weary, They shall walk and not faint.*

Isaiah 41:10. *Fear not, for I am with you; Be not dismayed, for I am your God. I will strengthen you, Yes, I will help you, I will uphold you with My righteous right hand.*

1 Chronicles 16:11 *Seek the LORD and His strength; Seek His face evermore!*

Exodus 15:2 *The LORD is my strength and song, And He has become my salvation; He is my God, and I will praise Him; My father's God, and I will exalt Him.*

Philippians 4:13 I can do all things through Christ who strengthens me.

Psalm 18:32-34 *It is* God who arms me with strength, And makes my way perfect. He makes my feet like the *feet of* deer, And sets me on my high places. He teaches my hands to make war, So that my arms can bend a bow of bronze.

1 Corinthians 10:13 *No temptation has overtaken you except such as is common to man; but God is faithful, who will not allow you to be tempted beyond what you are able, but with the temptation will also make the way of escape, that you may be able to bear it.*

Psalm 119:23 *Princes also sit and speak against me, But Your servant meditates on Your statutes.*

1 Samuel 30:6 *Now David was greatly distressed, for the people spoke of stoning him, because the soul of all the people was grieved, every man for his sons and his daughters. But David strengthened himself in the LORD his God.*

2 Timothy 4:17 *But the Lord stood with me and strengthened me, so that the message might be preached fully through me, and that all the Gentiles might hear. Also I was delivered out of the mouth of the lion.*

1 Peter 4:11 *If anyone speaks, let him speak as the oracles of God. If anyone ministers, let him do it as with the ability which God supplies, that in all things God may be glorified through Jesus Christ, to whom belong the glory and the dominion forever and ever. Amen.*

Joshua 1:9-11 *"Have I not commanded you? Be strong and of good courage; do not be afraid, nor be dismayed, for the LORD your God is with you wherever you go." Then Joshua commanded the officers of the people, saying "Pass through the camp and command the people, saying, 'Prepare provisions for yourselves, for within three days you will cross over this Jordan, to go in to possess the land which the LORD your God is giving you to possess."*

Genesis 22:1-3 *Now it came to pass after these things that God tested Abraham, and said to him, "Abraham!" And he said, "Here I am." Then He said, "Take now your son, your only son Isaac, whom you love, and go to the land of Moriah, and offer him there as a burnt offering on one of the mountains of which I shall tell you." So Abraham rose early in the morning and saddled his donkey, and took two of his young men with him, and Isaac his son; and he split the wood for the burnt offering, and arose and went to the place of which God had told him.*

Psalm 27:1 *The LORD is my light and my salvation; Whom shall I fear? The LORD is the strength of my life; Of whom shall I be afraid?*

Matthew 17:20 *So Jesus said to them, "Because of your unbelief; for assuredly, I say to you, if you have faith as a mustard seed, you will say to this mountain, 'Move from here to there,' and it will move; and nothing will be impossible for you.*

Mark 10:52 *Then Jesus said to him, "Go your way; your faith has made you well." And immediately he received his sight and followed Jesus on the road.*

Matthew 21:21 *So Jesus answered and said to them, "Assuredly, I say to you, if you have faith and do not doubt, you will not only do what was done to the fig tree, but also if you say to this mountain, 'Be removed and be cast into the sea,' it will be done.*

Meditate:
Matthew 18:18-20

Pray:
I am inviting all "Women on the R.U.N. for Jesus" to spend a minimum of one (1) hour daily in prayer.

Read: 2 Corinthians 12:7-10

What are some of the things in your life that help you feel content?

Are any of your goals frustrating you?

How do you apply Strength in your life?

CHAPTER 15

Relationships

Let's begin our lesson by opening our Bible to the Book Of *John* and <u>read</u> *Chapter 4 verses 1-42*.

St. John 4:1-42 will be the foundation that <u>Women on the R.U.N. for Jesus</u> is built on.

The first step in having a relationship is to have a relationship with Christ. With Christ in your life it becomes easier to deal with yourself and others. When you were born, the first person that you had contact with was your mother. Your mother holds an important part in a relationship with you. It is a nurturing love and as you grow up you look for that special love, that hug, that kiss, that smile; that unconditional love that only a mother can provide.

There is a greater relationship and that relationship is with Christ. *That if you confess with your mouth the Lord Jesus Christ and believe in your heart that God has raised Him from the dead, you will be saved.* Romans 10:9.

The Bible says, *Beloved, let us love one another, for love is of God; and everyone who loves is born of God and knows God. He who does not love does not know God, for God is love.* **1 John 4:7-8**

We love because He first loves us.

Karen and Sue were in a car and Sue was driving recklessly. Karen kept telling Sue, to slow down but she paid no attention to her. Sue continued her aggressive driving. Suddenly and without warning Sue lost control of the car and slammed into a tree. Karen was severely injured in the crash but somehow Sue escaped unharmed.

The doctors told Karen that she will never be able to use her arms and legs ever again. Karen's life appeared to be over. Her college education, plans to be a lawyer, marriage and family plans crushed. While on the other hand, Sue, the driver escaped without a scratch on her body. Every day, we as believers are faced with challenges. Maybe, some not as severe as Karen's but none-the-less we have a choice to walk according to our flesh or according to our Spirit.

The Bible says I cannot love God and hate my sister. If I love God I must love my sister also. The Bible also says that there is no fear in love, perfect love cast out all fear because fear involves torment. The Bible also says that God will not put on us more than we can bear.

Sue was totally shocked when Karen recovered and asked to see her.

It had been six (6) months since the accident and Sue asked her mother to accompany her to the rehabilitation facility to see Karen. When Sue walked into the room, the first thing she noticed was a big smile on

Karen's face. Tears began to roll down Sue's face. Before the words could leave Sue's mouth, Karen hushed her and spoke Matthew 18:18-20

Verily I say unto you, Whatsoever ye shall bind on earth shall be bound in heaven: and whatsoever ye shall loose on earth shall be loosed in heaven.

Again I say unto you, That if two of you shall agree on earth as touching anything that they shall ask, it shall be done for them of my Father which is in heaven.

For where two or three are gathered together in my name, there am I am in the midst of them.

As a Woman on the R.U.N. for Jesus, we are taught that our first relationship is with **J**esus then **O**thers, then **Y**ou, that is an acronym for **J O Y**. Don't look at someone's condition but the Bible says, *count it all Joy when you fall into various trials knowing that the testing of your faith produces patience but let patience have its perfect work, that you may be perfect and complete lacking nothing.* ***James 1:2-4***

My sister, the attitude of gratitude that Karen has towards Sue despite the circumstance is the kind of relationship we must have with everyone. We love because He first loved us. We cannot love Jesus and not love others because if we do we make Christ out to be a liar. The Bible says, *that any one that loves God and hates his brother, he is a liar, for he who does not love his brother whom he has seen, how he can love God whom he has not seen.* ***1 John 4:20***

Heavenly Father, I thank you. I thank you for giving me the wisdom to reach out to the world. Lord, I give you the praise. I give you the glory. I give you the honor. I worship you O Lord, for you are Sovereign in my life. You are Alpha and Omega. Lord, I thank you for directing my steps and having mercy on me because I know that I am not perfect. I need you Father, in my life each and every day. I know there is always something in me that you are working on and I surrender all to you. I acknowledge Father that I am not always pleasing to you, but because you are Wonderful, because you are Merciful, I know that your love is everlasting. I thank you Father for purifying my mind and using me in whatever way that is pleasing to you and forgive me Father for anything that is not pleasing to you. Lord, I thank you for allowing me to renew my mind each and every day so that I can hear more from you. I thank you for allowing me to forgive just like you forgive. Thank you for your J O Y and your peace. Remove my heart of stone and give me a heart of flesh. Renew a right spirit in me O God, starting today. I pray this prayer in Jesus name. Amen.

Meditate:
Matthew 18:18-20

Pray:
I am inviting all "Women on the R.U.N. for Jesus" to spend a minimum of one (1) hour daily in prayer.

Read:
Ephesians Chapter 4

CHAPTER 16

God's Benefits

Let's begin our lesson by opening our Bible to the Book Of *John* and <u>read</u> *Chapter 4 verses 1-42.*

St. John 4:1-42 will be the foundation that <u>Women on the R.U.N. for Jesus</u> is built on.

God's Benefits

When we come to know Christ, we acquire a wonderful benefit package. We are to enjoy all these benefits and apply them to our lives. We need to speak and receive the benefits of the Lord. The Lord is a forgiving God, He is a merciful God. He is a loving God. David said, we *are to Bless the Lord, O my soul, and Bless His holy name.* It is so wonderful to Bless His name and to Praise Him. Praise Him all day, every day. Having a relationship with God and spending time in the Word gives you the benefits that God has for you. *God rewards those who diligently seek Him*. It is so important in a Christian's life to give Him the thanks and praises. We must bless His name at all times.

In order to receive God's blessings and benefits we ought to practice doing the things that God requires us to do. Bless His name, Stay in the Word. Fellowship with one another and have the Agape Love that Jesus gives to us daily, His unconditional Love. Renew your mind and invite Him into your heart on a daily basis. Allow Him to remove anything in you that is not like Him. We sometimes do things our way and when we mess up we expect God to bless our mess. We have to acknowledge when we are wrong and go to God and speak to Him. He will forgive you. We want to receive His benefits so we should do what pleases Him. Speak His Word.

Here are the Blessings and Benefits that God gives us.

Psalm 103: Bless the LORD, O my soul; And all that is within me, *bless* His holy name! Bless the LORD, O my soul, And forget not all His benefits: Who forgives all your iniquities, Who heals all your diseases, Who redeems your life from destruction, Who crowns you with lovingkindness and tender mercies, Who satisfies your mouth with good *things, So that* your youth is renewed like the eagle's.

The LORD executes righteousness And justice for all who are oppressed. He made known His ways to Moses, His acts to the children of Israel. The LORD *is* merciful and gracious, Slow to anger, and abounding in mercy. He will not always strive *with us,* Nor will He keep *His anger* forever. He has not dealt with us according to our sins, Nor punished us according to our iniquities.

For as the heavens are high above the earth, *So* great is His mercy toward those who fear Him; As far as the east is from the west, *So* far has He removed our transgressions from us. As a father pities *his* children, *So* the Lord pities those who fear Him. For He knows our frame; He remembers that we *are* dust.

As for man, his days *are* like grass; As a flower of the field, so he flourishes. For the wind passes over it, and it is gone, And its place remembers it no more. But the mercy of the Lord *is* from everlasting to everlasting On those who fear Him, And His righteousness to children's children, To such as keep His covenant, And to those who remember His commandments to do them.

The Lord has established His throne in heaven, And His kingdom rules over all.

Bless the Lord, you His angels, Who excel in strength, who do His word, Heeding the voice of His word. Bless the Lord, all *you* His hosts, *You* ministers of His, who do His pleasure. Bless the Lord, all His works, In all places of His dominion.

Bless the Lord, O my soul!

Abraham

When God told Abraham to get out of your country, from his family and from his father's house to a land that He will show him. Abraham departed yes, but he took Lot and his wife Sarai. In **Genesis 11:31:** Terah took Abram and his grandson Lot, the son of Haran and his daughter-in-law Sarai, Abram's wife and went out with them from Ur to Chaldeans to go to the land of Canaan and came to Haran and dwelt there.

Abraham did like his father did. He took his possessions including his family and left. God did not tell him to take his family. He took his family. We are sometimes like this example, we know what God wants of us but we do it our way. We do not listen to what God tell us. Sometimes, we lose our blessings by not listening to the voice of God.

Even though Abraham did not do as God said he trusted God. In return he received many blessings from God. His faith grew stronger.

Let's look at the Promises to Abram:

Genesis 12: Now the LORD had said to Abram:

"Get out of your country, From your family And from your father's house, To a land that I will show you. I will make you a great nation; I will bless you And make your name great; And you shall be a blessing. I will bless those who bless you, And I will curse him who curses you; And in you all the families of the earth shall be blessed.

The Lord appeared to Abram many times and his faith grew stronger because he kept on trusting God. The Word of the Lord came to Abram in a vision saying, "Do not be afraid. I am your shield, your exceedingly great reward. **Genesis 15:1**

The Sign of the Covenant

Genesis 17: When Abram was ninety-nine years old, the LORD appeared to Abram and said to him, "I *am* Almighty God; walk before Me and be blameless. And I will make My covenant between Me and you, and will multiply you exceedingly." Then Abram fell on his face, and God talked with him, saying: "As for Me, behold, My covenant is with you, and you shall be a father of many nations. No longer shall your name be called Abram, but your name shall be Abraham; for I have made you a father of many nations.

We also can receive the many blessings from God. We ought to just step out in faith and trust and obey Him.

Meditate:
Matthew 18:18-20

Pray:
I am inviting all "Women on the R.U.N. for Jesus" to spend a minimum of one (1) hour daily in prayer.

Read:
Deut. 28-1-13

CHAPTER 17

Sin

Let's begin our lesson by opening our Bible to the Book Of *John* and __read__ *Chapter 4 verses 1-42*.

St. John 4:1-42 will be the foundation that __Women on the R.U.N.__ __for Jesus__ is built on.

Let's talk a little about sin. We know that Adam and Eve brought sin into this world. Jesus died for our sins. There are times when we do things that are not of God. We know what the Ten Commandments say, but for some reason or another we do not follow what God wants us to do.

Exodus 20:1-17 (NIV):

And God spoke all these words: "I am the LORD your God, who brought you out of Egypt, out of the land of slavery. "You shall have no other gods before me "You shall not make for yourself an image in the form of anything in heaven above or on the earth beneath or in the waters below. You shall not bow down to them or worship them; for I, the LORD your God, am a jealous God, punishing the children for the sin of the parents to the third and fourth generation of those who hate me, but showing love to a thousand generations of those who love me and keep my commandments. "You shall not misuse the name of the LORD your God, for the LORD will not hold anyone guiltless who misuses His name. "but the seventh day is a Sabbath to the LORD your God. On it you shall not do any work, neither you, nor your son or daughter, nor your male or female servant, nor your animals, nor any foreigner residing in your towns. For in six days the LORD made the heavens and the earth, the sea, and all that is in them, but He rested on the seventh day. Therefore the LORD blessed the Sabbath day and made it holy. "Honor your father and your mother, so that you may live long in the land the LORD your God is giving you. "You shall not murder. "You shall not commit adultery. "You shall not steal. "You shall not give false testimony against your neighbor. "You shall not covet your neighbor's house. You shall not covet your neighbor's wife, or his male or female servant, his ox or donkey, or anything that belongs to your neighbor."

There is so much sin in the world that we get caught up in doing things our way instead of God's way. The Bible talks about Adultery. Let's examine our heart. We want to do the right thing but we do the wrong thing because of our sin nature. We know Adultery is wrong but because of our flesh but we do it anyway.

In Matthew 5:27-30 (NIV) it says:

"You have heard that it was said, 'You shall not commit adultery.' But I tell you that anyone who looks at a woman lustfully has already committed adultery with her in his heart. If your right eye causes you to stumble, gouge it out and throw it away. It is better for you to lose one part of your body than for your whole body to be thrown into hell. And if your right hand causes you to stumble, cut it off and throw it away. It is better for you to lose one part of your body than for your whole body to go into hell.

It states clearly that anyone who looks at a woman lustfully has already committed adultery with her in his heart. When you come to a closer walk with God, you will not want to have any thought whatsoever in lusting with the eyes. Sin is Sin. If you see yourself getting caught up in this act, repent and do not allow any adulterous act to come into your heart.

The Bible also talks about loving your enemies. We get caught up in getting upset because someone has done us wrong. We get angry. We do not want to speak to that person. We do not want to forgive and we carry bitterness in our heart towards each other. In order for us to come clean with God we must forgive. We must not hold on to strive or any unforgiveness within our heart. God does not like that. God is a loving Father and forgiving Father. So we must love one another, no matter what the situation.

The Bible says: in Matthew 5:43-48 (NIV):

"You have heard that it was said, 'Love your neighbor and hate your enemy.' But I tell you, love your enemies and pray for those who persecute you, that you may be children of your Father in heaven. He causes His sun to rise on the evil and the good, and sends rain on the righteous and the unrighteous. If you love those who love you, what reward will you get? Are not even the tax collectors doing that? And if you greet only your own people, what are you doing more than others? Do not even pagans do that? [4]Be perfect, therefore, as your heavenly Father is perfect.

Let's talk about worry. Worry is also a sin. God expect us to trust Him in all things. There are times we lean unto our own understanding. We worry about this and we worry about that. Take for example, when children are not home at a certain time. We worry. When our spouse is not home we worry. When we don't have a job we worry. We worry about so many things.

But the Bible says clearly in Matthew 6:25-34 (NIV):

"Therefore I tell you, do not worry about your life, what you will eat or drink; or about your body, what you will wear. Is not life more than food and the body more than clothes? Look at the birds of the air; they do not sow or reap or store away in barns, and yet your heavenly Father feeds them. Are you not much more valuable than they? Can any one of you by worrying add a single hour to your life?

"And why do you worry about clothes? See how the flowers of the field grow. They do not labor or spin. Yet I tell you that not even Solomon in all his splendor was dressed like one of these. If that is how God clothes the grass of the field, which is here today and tomorrow is thrown into the fire, will he not much more clothe you—you of little faith? So do not worry, saying, 'What shall we eat?' or 'What shall we drink?' or 'What shall we wear?' For the pagans run after all these things, and your heavenly Father knows that you need them. But seek first His kingdom and His righteousness, and all these things will be given to you as well. Therefore do not worry about tomorrow, for tomorrow will worry about itself. Each day has enough trouble of its own.

Let's leave our cares in God's hand. He will never leave us nor forsake us. Receive and believe.

Meditate:
Matthew 18:18-20

Pray:
I am inviting all "Women on the R.U.N. for Jesus" to spend a minimum of one (1) hour daily in prayer.

Read:
Romans 6

CHAPTER 18

The Tongue

Let's begin our lesson by opening our Bible to the Book Of *John* and <u>read</u> *Chapter 4 verses 1-42.*

St. John 4:1-42 will be the foundation that <u>Women on the R.U.N. for Jesus</u> is built on.

Let's talk a little about the tongue. Sometimes, words are so powerful. We say things without thinking. We hurt others with our mouth by speaking out the wrong words. We must examine ourselves and begin to talk in a way that Jesus will like us to speak. We must be careful with the tongue. The tongue is a weapon. Before we speak, we must be "quick to listen, and slow to speak". We must practice this quote.

When we get upset, we call this one and we call that one. We yell, we scream. We say harmful words out of our mouth. We get vindictive and lie and treat each other disrespectfully. What a big mess. We can never feel good within and must examine ourselves and remove ourselves from these wrong and evil thoughts. We must say to ourselves, 'What would Jesus say? We must put away all these wrong thoughts and replace them with kind words of love and admiration towards one other. Practice becomes perfect. Yes, practice each day and work on your behavior and you will become more and more like Jesus.

There was a time in my life when I would get angry, very emotional and upset over every little thing. I would let my emotions get out of control and I would respond angrily with a loud voice. This never made me feel good but because of the love of Jesus within me I began to overcome these emotions. Over the years I got better although I still find myself getting a bit emotional at times, I know that I can go to Jesus; repent, if necessary and move on with the peace of God inside of me.

We cannot say we love God and hate our brother. We cannot walk around carrying bitterness and hate towards one another. We laugh with one another and as soon as our back is turned, we gossip about one another, speaking lies and hurtful words. Let's not get quiet now. Do I have a witness in the House? When you hear something about someone, you get on the phone and call Jim or Susie and start to gossip about that brother or sister. This is sin. Sin is totally wrong. We must be slow to speak, quick to listen and ready to respond in an attitude of love.

The Bible says in 1 John 4:17-21:

Love has been perfected among us in this: that we may have boldness in the day of judgment; because as He is, so are we in this world. There is no fear in love; but perfect love casts out fear, because fear involves torment. But he who fears has not been made perfect in love. We love Him because He first loved us. If someone says, "I love God," and hates his brother, he is a liar; for he who does not love his brother whom he has seen, how can he love God whom he has not seen? And this commandment we have from Him: that he who loves God *must* love his brother also.

Here what the Bible says about the tongue in James 3:

My brethren, let not many of you become teachers, knowing that we shall receive a stricter judgment. For we all stumble in many things. If anyone does not stumble in word, he *is* a perfect man, able also to bridle the whole body. Indeed we put bits in horses' mouths that they may obey us, and we turn their whole body. Look also at ships: although they are so large and are driven by fierce winds, they are turned by a very small rudder wherever the pilot desires. Even so the tongue is a little member and boasts great things. See how great a forest a little fire kindles! And the tongue *is* a fire, a world of iniquity. The tongue is so set among our members that it defiles the whole body, and sets on fire the course of nature; and it is set on fire by hell. For every kind of beast and bird, of reptile and creature of the sea, is tamed and has been tamed by mankind. But no man can tame the tongue. *It is* an unruly evil, full of deadly poison. With it we bless our God and Father, and with it we curse men, who have been made in the similitude of God. Out of the same mouth proceed blessing and cursing. My brethren, these things ought not to be so. Does a spring send forth fresh *water* and bitter from the same opening? Can a fig tree, my brethren, bear olives, or a grapevine bear figs? Thus no spring yields both salt water and fresh. Who *is* wise and understanding among you? Let him show by good conduct *that* his works *are done* in the meekness of wisdom. But if you have bitter envy and self-seeking in your hearts, do not boast and lie against the truth. This wisdom does not descend from above, but *is* earthly, sensual, demonic. For where envy and self-seeking *exist,* confusion and every evil thing *are* there. But the wisdom that is from above is first pure, then peaceable, gentle, willing to yield, full of mercy and good fruits, without partiality and without hypocrisy. Now the fruit of righteousness is sown in peace by those who make peace.

Meditate:
Matthew 18:18-20

Pray:
I am inviting all "Women on the R.U.N. for Jesus" to spend a minimum of one (1) hour daily in prayer.

Read:
James Chapter 3

CHAPTER 19

Healing

Let's begin our lesson by opening our Bible to the Book Of *John* and <u>read</u> *Chapter 4 verses 1-42.*

St. John 4:1-42 will be the foundation that <u>Women on the R.U.N. for Jesus </u>is built on.

We often hear the Bible verse, by His stripes we are healed. God's Word is alive. There are times in each of our lives we do not apply the healing scriptures. We use medicine to cure whatever sickness or illness that comes upon us. But God's Word says that we are healed. We have to believe Him. There are times we have to go to doctors, but God is the one who give doctors the wisdom to use the medicine when it is needed. But when you put your trust in the Word of God and believe that His Word is Power. He is the only one that can Heal us.

Let's go back into the Bible in Matthew 8:1:13 (NIV):

Jesus Heals a Man with Leprosy

When Jesus came down from the mountainside, large crowds followed Him. A man with leprosy came and knelt before Him and said, "Lord, if you are willing, you can make me clean. "Jesus reached out His hand and touched the man. "I am willing," He said. "Be clean!" Immediately he was cleansed of his leprosy. Then Jesus said to him, "See that you don't tell anyone. But go, show yourself to the priest and offer the gift Moses commanded, as a testimony to them."

The Faith of the Centurion

When Jesus had entered Capernaum, a centurion came to him, asking for help. "Lord," he said, "my servant lies at home paralyzed, suffering terribly. "Jesus said to him, "Shall I come and heal him? "The centurion replied, "Lord, I do not deserve to have you come under my roof. But just say the word, and my servant will be healed. For I myself am a man under authority, with soldiers under me. I tell this one, 'Go,' and he goes; and that one, 'Come,' and he comes. I say to my servant, 'Do this,' and he does it." When Jesus heard this, he was amazed and said to those following Him, "Truly I tell you, I have not found anyone in Israel with such great faith. I say to you that many will come from the east and the west, and will take their places at the feast with Abraham, Isaac and Jacob in the kingdom of heaven. But the subjects of the kingdom will be thrown outside, into the darkness, where there will be weeping and gnashing of teeth. "Then Jesus said to the centurion, "Go! Let it be done just as you believed it would." And his servant was healed at that moment. This centurion had great faith in Jesus. Jesus was pleased by his faith so he was healed. How many of us have this faith that Jesus can heal us? We have to continue trusting and believing. For God will always show in His Spirit that you are healed in Jesus Name.

Let's see more of whom Jesus healed in the Bible in Matthew 9:18-38 (NIV):

Jesus Raises a Dead Girl and Heals a Sick Woman

While he was saying this, a synagogue leader came and knelt before Him and said, "My daughter has just died. But come and put your hand on her, and she will live." Jesus got up and went with him, and so did his disciples. Just then a woman who had been subject to bleeding for twelve years came up behind Him and touched the edge of His cloak. She said to herself, "If I only touch His cloak, I will be healed. "Jesus turned and saw her. "Take heart, daughter," He said, "your faith has healed you." And the woman was healed at that moment. When Jesus entered the synagogue leader's house and saw the noisy crowd and people playing pipes, He said, "Go away. The girl is not dead but asleep." But they laughed at Him. After the crowd had been put outside, He went in and took the girl by the hand, and she got up. News of this spread through all that region.

Jesus Heals the Blind and the Mute

As Jesus went on from there, two blind men followed Him, calling out, "Have mercy on us, Son of David! "When He had gone indoors, the blind men came to Him, and He asked them, "Do you believe that I am able to do this? "Yes, Lord," they replied. Then He touched their eyes and said, "According to your faith let it be done to you"; and their sight was restored. Jesus warned them sternly, "See that no one knows about this." But they went out and spread the news about Him all over that region. While they were going out, a man who was demon-possessed and could not talk was brought to Jesus. And when the demon was driven out, the man who had been mute spoke. The crowd was amazed and said, "Nothing like this has ever been seen in Israel. "But the Pharisees said, "It is by the prince of demons that He drives out demons." Jesus went through all the towns and villages, teaching in their synagogues, proclaiming the good news of the kingdom and healing every disease and sickness. When He saw the crowds, He had compassion on them, because they were harassed and helpless, like sheep without a shepherd. Then He said to his disciples, "The harvest is plentiful but the workers are few.

It is so wonderful to see how God healed so many people. He can also do it for us if we apply His healing scriptures to our lives. God will continue to heal us spirit, soul and body. He lives in us and He lives with us. We must thank Jesus for our healing each and every day. Amen.

Meditate:
Matthew 18:18-20

Pray:
I am inviting all "Women on the R.U.N.for Jesus" to spend a minimum of one (1) hour daily in prayer.

Read:
Psalm 103:1-5

CHAPTER 20

Testimonies

Let's begin our lesson by opening our Bible to the Book Of *John* and <u>read</u> *Chapter 4 verses 1-42.*

St. John 4:1-42 will be the foundation that <u>Women on the R.U.N. for Jesus</u> is built on.

Women are struggling with issues today. In order to be an "Overcomer", invite Jesus into your Heart and allow Him to work in your life. Be an "Overcomer" and ask God to remove anything in you that is not like Him. Just invite the Holy Spirit into your life and He will fix it and receive the Joy of the Lord deep within. His Joy is your strength. ***Nehemiah 8:10***

If someone says wrong words to you such as BAD and STUPID; DO NOT RECEIVE THEM! We can choose to use negative or positive words in our conversations. But always remember, negative words that hurt others do not please God. As a Christian, I have learned to guard my tongue because from out of it can come curses or blessings. You see, when you speak negatively, you get negative results and when you speak positive, you get positive results. "Remember death and life are in the power of the tongue.*" Proverbs 18:21*

When I came to know Christ, it was not very easy. I was struggling with many issues in my world of sin. I was sick and tired of people telling me what to do; criticizing and making fun of me. You see, I was bound up by sin but as I began to know who I am in Christ, a child who is unconditionally loved by God; I allowed the Holy Spirit to have His way. I bound up the works of the flesh and released the peace of the Lord that passes all understanding into my life. "Assuredly, I say to you, whatever you bind on earth will be bound in heaven and whatever you loose on earth will be loosed in heaven". *Matthew 18:18*

I will always depend on my Savior. I will continue Lifting Him up. I will continue being drawn to Him. I will kneel at the feet of my soon coming King and give Him all the glory, because He is worthy to be praised. "Worthy is the Lamb!" *Revelation 6:12*

There are times when I am praising God, I reach out my hand to Him. I say Yes, Lord, here I am. I feel His presence like a gentle breeze, sweeping across my face and touching my heart and saying: *"My child, it's all right."* We have to give Him All the Glory. I said All, not some.

ALL THE GLORY!

God has shown me that His Word never changes. He said, I will separate you from whence you came and put new Christians in your life. He says that I have to forsake my past and the people that I let in. He says He will give me a new family in Christ, and that's what He has done.

I believe God is showing me that I have been called out. I have been separated from the world.

I know He wants to use me to deliver His Word by way of teaching.

I've learned that God places us in positions to shine the light of Christ in our daily walk. We encounter different aspects of life all coming from God but when we see how He manifests Himself in us, we have to acknowledge that Christ alone is God. Women on the R.U.N. reflects the love of Christ in us by nourishing others. We reflect on the Word, and we reach out to those who do not have a personal relationship with God.

God has taken me to another level of awareness: new journey, new story to tell, blessings beyond myself. God wants to show me how to stand through all my adversities when I thought they would kill me.

But I'm still here! Yes, it was painful and even now still is, but I'm working through my pain. Fear and Doubt conquered, Faith and Belief in God has taken its place first and foremost in my heart and soul. Everything I do now must go through Jesus. I'm having a love relationship with the Divine now. God is my Friend, my Father and my Counselor. I can do nothing without Him, I'm better now.

I've learned to be still. Put my thoughts before my actions. Be still. Think before speaking. Be still. Just keep my connection with my Lord and Savior. Always open. Listen for His directions. I want to see my soul free of passed pain. Forget my failures. Free my soul from judgment. Forget the past and move into my new journey.

I want to embrace whatever God wants me to do now, for I'm sure it is for my good. I want God to cleanse my heart, transform my mind. Return me to my original self, my true life that He created; a life of purity, peace, love, joy and happiness. My response starting today will reflect Christ. I will be humble, a woman that shines with the light that comes from being in love with God and not the world. I want to love everyone, whether, good or bad, knowing that with Christ Jesus I am never alone, ever.

There were times I just wanted to be alone. There was so much hurt built up in me that I did not want to associate myself with anyone. I felt lost, and bitter. I did not want to be around anyone. I realized that we all have some pride in us. I had a lot of pride in me and when something bothers me and I cannot express myself in the way I would like to, pride steps in. If it was not for God who I continue to have a relationship with, I would have been doing what I want to do. "But God". I said "But God". I always invite Him into my heart and renew my mind so I can get rid of all the wrong thoughts. People will sometimes try to discourage you from doing what God has called you to do. In order to do your assignment from God, you have to listen to God and not people. If God says Yes! It's Yes! You do not have to go and ask another for an answer.

I have come a long way with God. I still have not got everything right with God. I am still depending on Him. I am still waiting on Him. Altogether, I know for certain, because I am not perfect, I will continue

Lifting My God Higher, Praising Him for all what He has done and making Him First in my Life.

While attending a conference in Manhattan, NY, I sat next to a young woman who caught my attention. I notice she was enjoying the Christian conference. She looked at me where I was seated in back of her and asked me. (Ms. Do you have two dollar?) I will like to take the train back to the shelter but have no travelling monies. I took out the $2.00 and gave it to her. She thanked me. She started telling me about how her family was not kind to her and some of her problems that she was encountering. To make a long story short, after the show, I started on my way to go to the subway. She walked in my direction to the train station. I asked, Are you going to take the train? She acted surprised.

She said, "No!" I knew in the spirit something was not clicking, however all I could do was ask the Holy Spirit into her heart. I was glad that I was able to be of assistance to her. The bottom line is this, we have to show love in every situation. God already knows. We have to continue showing and giving love. God will do the rest.

I will bless the Lord, and give Him glory,

Oh I will bless His name and give Him glory.

Oh I will bless you Lord, and give you all the glory, Oh I will bless your name and give you all the glory. Oh I will bless you Lord, and give you all the glory, O I will bless your name and give you all the glory. Yes, I'll give you all the glory. Yes, I''ll give you all the glory.

You see, I will continue blessing His name. Sometimes, we give man the praise. Flattering words, impressing others when we should be giving God the glory and Praising His name.

Jill had an interview for an office assistant position in a doctor's office in the city. Jill had been going on many interviews but the door has not been open as she expected it to be. On her arrival at the office she was told by the doctor that the receptionist will help her. After a few minutes the receptionist escorted her into one of the rooms in the office and was asked a few questions regarding the position. Although, Jill knew the aspects of the position that was outlined to her, she felt a little uneasy with some questions being asked. However, the receptionist told her that they will be interviewing other candidates and this is the first of two interviews and will be calling back candidates that will be selected to come back.

You see, when Jill got home she called the office and let the receptionist know that she enjoyed the interview and she is hoping to be called back. She was impressing the receptionist with positive words, in order to get the job.

God is the only one that gets the glory. Man does not get the glory. What God has for you, He will make sure you will get it. If it is not an open door, it is not His will. We have to keep thanking and Praising Him and giving Him the glory. In His time not our time. He will continue providing for you until the right door is open. Keep Praising Him, thanking Him and giving Him the glory.

Jesus said come just as you are. He said He will never leave us nor forsake us. When Jesus is calling, He is not looking for you to put on make-up, wigs, eye shadow or a fancy dress. When you were born, you did not come with a wig, you did not come with make-up. You did not come with a fancy dress. You came naked into this world.

I was watching a TV show some years back. There was a lady who was interviewed. She said, she had to look beautiful for her husband. At night she would wear a lot of makeup. She wore this makeup every night. Her husband never saw her without makeup. The interviewer then asked her to take off the makeup. She was scared to take the makeup off. After taking the makeup off, fear was within her but she had to come to her senses that it was her husband she is pleasing. She is a beautiful person without the makeup but she was conscious of herself and wanted to please her husband.

Society is messed up. When you are living in the flesh, we want to please man, but when you come to know Jesus Christ, the only one you have to please is God. Of course, we should look beautiful but we are to love ourselves and know that God is beautiful. God made us and we are beautiful people. *GOD DID NOT MAKE JUNK. I SAID, GOD DID NOT MAKE JUNK.* God made everything good so we must feel beautiful in His sight. It took a lot of courage to see herself beautiful and to know that she is beautiful.

As you read this story this will change how you treat others who stick by you through all that you go through no matter what. Amen! There was a blind girl who hated herself because she was blind. She hated every one except her loving boyfriend. He was always there for her. She told her boyfriend one day that, "if she could only see the world, she will marry him" so one day someone donated a pair of eyes to her. When the bandages came off, she was able to see everything including her boyfriend. The boyfriend asked her, "now that u can see the world, will u marry me?" the girl looked at her boyfriend and noticed that he was blind. The sight of his closed eyelids shocked her. She hadn't expected that. The

thought of looking at him for the rest of her life led her to refuse to marry him. Her boyfriend left her in tears. And days later he sent a message saying, "take good care of your eyes my dear, because they were mine"! Amen!

I've moved on with Christ.

You see, I have had some good times and I had some bad times,

I have had some rough times and I had some smooth times,

I had some happy times and I had some sad times,

But through it all I have learned to trust and depend on Jesus.

I am a Woman on the R.U.N. for Jesus.

Meditate:
Matthew 18:18-20

Pray:
I am inviting all "Women on the R.U.N. for Jesus" to spend a minimum of one (1) hour daily in prayer.

Read:
Hebrews 11-5

AFTER WORDS

<u>The Presence of God is Everywhere</u>

While on our way to Church on Sunday morning, we headed out to one of the nearby local churches. The church is the daughter church of another church in another city. As we entered the church, I didn't see a lot of people. The crowd was extremely small, not the average crowd of people that I am using to seeing at a service. However, as I looked around, I asked my husband, "Do you feel the presence of God here?" He said, "Yes!" I know the presence of God is everywhere once we focus on Him. I know we have to feel His presence wherever we go. My husband said, "this is where God wants us to be today."

You see, when you leave your home, you should leave with the presence of God. The presence of God is always with you. Amen.

What happened in that space of time was amazing. God started to speak to me. He said, "*Where two of three are gathered together in my name, I am in the midst.*" I said, "Yes Lord." Then I received confirmation from my husband who looked at me and said, "God said, where two or three are gathered together, there I am in the midst." God changed my thoughts and I began to experience a deeper presence of Him.

The Choir was small but as soon as they started singing, the glory of the Lord filled the Temple. The Holy Spirit fell on everyone. We were all standing, praising and worshipping our God. A dear sister came over to me and held my hand and brought me out onto the floor while the choir was singing and rejoicing in the Lord. We were just enjoying the presence of God, glorifying Him in praise and worship. Halleluiah, Jesus!

God put me in the atmosphere where He wanted me to be, God said," this is where I want you to be." The rest of the worship was a blessing, seeing everyone enjoying the presence of God. We should focus on Him and His presence not the building, God is Omniscient; His presence is everywhere.

Prayers to the Father

Father, I come before you with open arms, lifting you higher. Magnifying your name. Father, I ask that you touch the children of this world. Every child, Father. The children are in your care, Father. Touch their lives, Father. Direct them and show them the right way, Lord. O Lord, I thank you for what you are doing in these children's lives. Lord, sometimes, they don't know, but you know Father. Cover them all with your blood, going out and coming in, Father. Touch the parents, mother and father of these children. Keep them strong. O Lord, we need you to keep our children safe and keep them in your care. We thank you for covering them with your blood and when they leave the house Father, they will go and come back safe in your care. Lord we thank you for watching over all children and cover each and every household, in Jesus Precious Name. Amen.

Father, here I am again. It's me O Lord. I renew my mind again Lord. Lord, you are so Wonderful, so Marvelous, so Beautiful. Lord you are Love. Thank you Lord for another day of life, just to say thank you Father. This is the day that you have made and I will rejoice and be glad in it. Lord, I lift up every man, woman and child to you in the Name of Jesus. Touch Lord. Cleanse Lord. I ask your salvation for this whole world Father. Lord, I lift up each and every Nation to you. Salvation for this world Lord. Heal this land Lord. Lord, I thank you for all that you have done and I thank you in Jesus Name. Amen

Heavenly Father, I come to you once again. Father God, I thank you for another day. For this is the day that you have made and I will rejoice in it Father. As I renew my mind, I invite you once again into my heart Father. Father, I magnify your Name. I Worship you Lord. I give you all the Praises, for you deserve the Glory. I thank you for saving souls Father. I thank you for keeping me. I thank you for Loving me Unconditionally Father. You are a real God. You are a Good God. All the time you are Good Father. I thank you for your abundant Blessings. I Lift you up in the Name of Jesus, Father. I Love you Father and I adore you Father, in Jesus Precious Name. Amen.

Glory, Glory, Glory. Thank you, Thank you Father. Lord I come to you once again Praising your name. Have your way Lord, Have your way. Search me O God and if there is anything that is not like you, remove it Father. Lord I thank you for saving souls, I lift up every man, woman and child to you Lord. Lord touch them. Save the children of this world Father God. Lord touch hearts. Father God, I lift up each and every Nation to you, I lift up the Pastors, Leaders, those in Authority, the sick, those who are suffering, Father. I ask in Jesus Name to heal this land. By your stripes we are all healed in Jesus Name.

Joy In the Spirit

Praise God from whom all blessings flow . . . . . .

Let me speak a little about joy; do not let anyone steal your joy.

When you get up in the morning and start to praise God; do not let anyone steal your joy.

When you get on your knees and start crying out to the Lord; do not let anyone steal your joy.

When you were fasting and praying, not only for yourself, but for your loved ones; do not let anyone steal your joy.

Do not allow others to get you upset; remember how you got your joy.

Remember, the devil comes to steal, kill and destroy; do not allow the enemy to attack you.

Submit to God and resist the enemy and he must flee. (James 4:7)

There are people that want to steal your joy—for any reason. They don't like seeing you happy or seeing you prosper. Maybe they are feeling down and want you to feel the same. Keep your eyes focused on Jesus and do not let anyones' negativity upset you.

Be strong in the Lord and in the power of His might. (Ephesians 6:10)

The Joy of the Lord is our strength. (Nehemiah 8:10)

We can overcome times of joylessness. Some of the people in the Bible overcame depression.

In Job 33:26 Job said, *if we pray and remember our blessings, God will restore us to joy and righteousness.*

In Psalm 19:8 David wrote, the study of God's Word brings us joy. Amen.

It's Christ Church

*Then the man and his wife heard the sound of the LORD GOD AS HE WAS WALKING in the garden **in the cool of the day,** and they hid from the LORD God among the trees of the garden. (Genesis 3:8-9) But the LORD God called to the man, "Where are you?"* The coolest time of day would actually be just before the sun comes up and is the time that **Jehovah Elohim** is walking in the garden working to enlarge your territory, spiritually.

About midnight *Paul and Silas were praying and singing hymns to God, and the other prisoners were listening to them. Suddenly there was such a violent earthquake that the foundations of the prison were shaken.* ***At once*** *all the prison doors flew open, and everyone's chains came loose. The jailer woke up, and when he saw the prison doors open, he drew his sword and was about to kill himself because he thought the prisoners had escaped. But Paul shouted, "Don't harm yourself! We are all here!" The jailer **called for lights,** rushed in and fell trembling before Paul and Silas. He then brought them out and asked, "Sirs, **what must I do to be saved?"** They replied, **"Believe in the Lord Jesus, and you will be saved—you and your household.** "Then they spoke the word of the Lord to him and to all the others in his house. At that hour of the night the jailer took them and washed their wounds; then immediately he and his entire household were baptized. The jailer brought them into his house and set a meal before them; **he was filled with joy because he had come to believe in God—he and his whole household!** When it was **daylight,** the magistrates sent their officers to the jailer with the order: "Release those men." The jailer told Paul, "The magistrates have ordered that you and Silas be released. Now you can leave. **Go in peace**.* (Acts 16:25-36)

The Word of God is clear. If you want your territory enlarged you must rise early and meet Him in the Garden in front of the Tree of Life and eat freely so at midnight you can pray and sing hymns to Him so you can possess that territory. The enemy will tempt you so you will have to hide in His Presence but the Bible says, *Submit yourselves, then, to God. Resist the devil, and he will flee from you.* (James 4:7) Then at midnight you can pray, sing and shout like the Israelites did at Jericho and shake the foundation of every spiritual stronghold, every wile of the devil and watch those walls, those shackles, those chains and any other thing that has you bound, come loose. And the glory of the Lord will fill this place! Souls will be saved and sinners will be filled with joy because they have chosen to believe the Truth and rejected the lie. The church will be healthy and whole for the first time in this generation with Christ as the Head and we as the body. Hallelujah- Jesus! . . . . **it's Christ's Church!**

Father, in the name of Jesus, show Yourself strong Lord. Touch the hearts and lives of everyone reading or has read this book and give them a passion for Your people.

Oh God, show us your glory like you did Moses like you did Elijah. Oh God, give us a glimpse of Heaven right here on Earth. Break all generational curses and tear down every spiritual stronghold that keeps Your children from seeing the light of Your glory. Oh God, we pray today that You will hear us today and reverse the curse that has us chained, shackled and bound. Oh God, we love You. We need You. We believe You. Fill us with joy unspeakable and Your perfect peace which passes all understanding. Hear Your people, oh God and bless us expediently, in Jesus name we pray. Amen and Amen

(Rev. Tarrent-Arthur Henry)

Finally, I will continue to allow God to work in my life. I will continue listening to that still small voice and allow the Holy Spirit to work through me. Don't let the devil steal your joy. Remember, the devil is a liar, a deceiver and evil, so continue to stomp on him. Continue to grow in Christ . . . . . for He will never leave you nor forsake you. His Word says so. Believe Him and Receive Him in Jesus Name. We should always be ready to lift up each other in the Body of Christ and pray for the unsaved loved ones so that they may also come to have a relationship with God Almighty.

Accept Jesus as Lord and Savior

If you like to dedicate or to re-dedicate your life to Christ
Because of what you read in this book
Please say this aloud with me:

Lord Jesus, I believe that you are God.
I believe that you went to the cross to die for me.
I believe that you rose from the dead . . . .
Lord Jesus, I am a sinner and I want to repent of my sin, right now.
Lord Jesus, come into my heart and take control of my life.
Right now . . . Jesus . . . Right now . . . . .
In Your precious name I pray, Amen.

ABOUT AUTHOR

Helen is the Co-founder of A&H Ministries, together with her husband, Rev. Arthur Henry, founder. Together, they are being called by God to reach out to the lost souls all around the world, letting them know about the love of the Lord Jesus Christ. She is also the author of "Telling It All From the Heart" (Authorhouse).

Helen is available for book signings, and speaking engagements.

To Contact the Author:

Email Address: Helenjc08@yahoo.com
Website: www.Helench.org

MY MOTHER

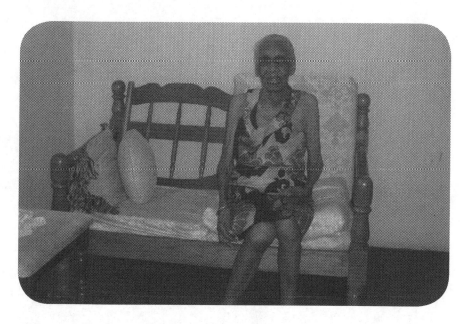

When my husband Arthur and I, visited my mother and sister in Trinidad, West Indies; I knew that God had me on an assignment. My mother celebrated her 92nd birthday on October 7th, and I was happy to be there to enjoy this day with her. Wearing the beautiful dress I put on her for her Birthday meant a lot to me. To dress her, comb her hair and make her look nice was a joy for me. Thank you Jesus.

Helping my mother and seeing that she could not walk as fast as she used to, was not a good feeling for me, but on the other hand washing her face and body was a joy for me. While I was doing this, my mother said to me, "God will bless you." I knew God's presence was there.

She said again, while I was helping her put her clothes on, "God will bless you." I just looked at her with teary eyes, and in the midst of my thoughts, I said "Thank you Jesus for being here with us."

My prayer to God was having a home attendant in the night and a home attendant in the day, and God put things in order. You see, God connects you with the right sources and that's what He did in the time I spent in Trinidad with my mother and sister.

The highest honor you can give God is to believe His Word, and that's what Faith is. Faith believes what God has said above anything else and there is nothing in the world that God does not want you to have. The Bible tells us to *Honor your father and your mother, that your days may be long upon the land which the Lord your God is giving you.* (Exodus 20:12) I believe that because my mother taught me how to love God and His Word, God has given her a long life.

My mother is a "Woman on the R.U.N. for Jesus" (Righteous, Uplifting, Nourishing).